A PERFORMER'S GUIDE TO MUSIC *of* THE Romantic Period

Series Editor
Anthony Burton

The Associated Board of
the Royal Schools of Music

First published in 2002 by

The Associated Board of the Royal Schools of Music (Publishing) Limited

24 Portland Place, London W1B 1LU, United Kingdom

© 2002 by The Associated Board of the Royal Schools of Music

ISBN 1 86096 194 0

AB 2766

A CIP catalogue for this book is available from The British Library.

Design and formatting by Geoffrey Wadsley

Music origination by Jack Thompson

Printed in England by Halstan & Co. Ltd, Amersham, Bucks

Contents

Illustrations

Notes on the Contributors

Sir Roger Norrington has been one of the leading pioneers of historical performance practice for many years, through the performances and recordings he has conducted with the Schütz Choir, the London Baroque Players, the London Classical Players and the Orchestra of the Age of Enlightenment. He is also in worldwide demand as a conductor of symphony orchestras, and is chief conductor of the Stuttgart Radio Symphony Orchestra.

Hugh Macdonald is Avis Blewett Professor of Music at Washington University, St Louis. Born in England, he taught at both Oxford and Cambridge Universities before moving to the United States in 1987. He is general editor of the New Berlioz Edition, and has written books on Berlioz and Skryabin as well as articles on a wide range of other musical topics.

Clive Brown is professor of applied musicology in the University of Leeds. His books include *Classical and Romantic Performing Practice 1750–1900* and the standard biography of Louis Spohr, together with a study of Mendelssohn now in preparation. He has also published many articles and critical editions. His work on performance practice is informed by his own experience as a violinist.

Roy Howat is well known as a pianist, writer and editor. He has recorded a wide range of solo and chamber music, including a series of the complete solo piano music of Debussy. He has written a study of Debussy, and edited volumes of music by Debussy, Fauré and Chabrier. He is AHRB Fellow in Creative and Performing Arts at the Royal College of Music, London.

David Goode was organ scholar at King's College, Cambridge, and after winning top prizes at competitions in St Albans and Calgary became sub-organist of Christ Church, Oxford. He now has a busy career as a teacher, international recitalist and recording artist.

Robin Stowell studied musicology at Cambridge University and the violin at the Royal Academy of Music in London, and has since combined his academic musical interests with an active performing career. He holds a professorship at the University of Wales, Cardiff, where he has taught since 1976, and plays regularly with numerous orchestras and chamber ensembles. He is the author of books and articles on string performance practice, and co-editor of the Cambridge Handbooks to the Historical Performance of Music.

Trevor Herbert is professor of music at The Open University, and has played trombone with most of the major British orchestras, as well as ensembles including The Taverner Players and The Wallace Collection. He has written extensively on brass instruments, his publications including *The Cambridge Companion to Brass Instruments*, which he edited with John Wallace, and *The British Brass Band: A Musical and Social History*.

David Mason is known internationally as a soloist and accompanist on piano, harpsichord and fortepiano. In the early part of his career he also studied voice, sang as an oratorio soloist, and researched bel canto techniques. This unusual range of experience led him to begin teaching singers, and he is now in great demand as a singing teacher in Spain (his adopted home), the Netherlands and London. He has written many articles on historical singing styles and techniques.

Robert Pascall studied at Oxford University, then taught at the University of Nottingham for thirty years, the last ten as professor and head of music; he is now professor and head of music at the University of Wales, Bangor. He has published editions of works by Brahms, and many analytical and historical studies of nineteenth- and twentieth-century music. He is also active as an organist and conductor.

Anthony Burton studied music at Cambridge University, and worked as an arts administrator in New England and in Manchester before spending fifteen years as a music producer and manager for BBC Radio 3. He is now a freelance broadcaster and writer, covering a wide range of musical subjects. He was guest artistic director of the 2001 Spitalfields Festival in east London.

Acknowledgements

Acknowledgement for permission to reproduce illustrations and music examples is due to the following:

Illustrations
The British Library, London: Figs 4.1, 4.2, 4.3
Courtesy of Cyfarthfa Castle Museum and Art Gallery: Fig. 5.4
© Copyright Edinburgh University Collection of Historic Musical
    Instruments. Reproduced by kind permission. Photography – Antonia
    Reeve Photography, Edinburgh: Figs 5.1, 5.2
Reproduced by kind permission of C. Hurst & Co. Publishers Ltd from M. I.
    Wilson, *Organ Cases of Western Europe* (London: C. Hurst, 1979): Fig. 3.2
Lebrecht Music Collection: Fig. 1.2
Öffentliche Kunstsammlung Basel, Kunstmuseum/Martin Bühler: Fig. 1.3
© Copyright Steinway & Sons. Reproduced by kind permission: Fig. 3.1

Music examples
Bibliothèque Nationale de France, Paris: Ex. 7.1
© 1909 – Joint ownership Redfield and Nordice. Exclusive representation
    Editions Durand, Paris (France). Reproduced by permission of Editions
    Durand, Paris/G. Ricordi & Co. (London) Ltd: Ex. 3.3
Copyright © 1924 by Carl Fischer, Inc. Copyright renewed. All rights
    assigned to Carl Fischer, LLC. International copyright secured. All rights
    reserved. Used with permission: Ex. 4.2
Reproduced by permission of Editions Hamelle, Paris/United Music
    Publishers Ltd: Ex. 6.16
Reproduced by permission of Editions Max Eschig, Paris/United Music
    Publishers Ltd: Exx. 3.2, 3.6
Gesellschaft der Musikfreunde, Wien: Ex. 7.2
Österreichische NationalBibliothek, Wien: Ex. 2.2

Front and back covers
Chopin Playing the Piano in Prince Radziwill's Salon, 1887, by Hendrik
    Siemiradzki (1843–1902): Private Collection/Berko Fine Paintings,
    Knokke-Zoute, Belgium/Bridgeman Art Library.

Thanks are also expressed to Lance Whitehead and Jenny Nex for helpful
information on the topic of keyboard compass, Table 3.1.

General Notes

Throughout this book, note pitches are described using the Helmholtz system:

In the captions to the music examples, the date refers to composition unless given in brackets, in which case it is the date of publication or, in the case of stage works, first performance.

The symbol ⑩ is a cross-reference to the accompanying CD and the Notes on the CD on pp. 107–10.

Anthony Burton

Preface

What does it mean if you have played or sung a piece, and a friend, or a teacher, or an adjudicator, comments: 'That had a good sense of style'; or maybe 'That wasn't very stylish'? It means that the piece was performed with – or without – an understanding of how the composer would have expected it to sound at the time it was written. And it is to help you to find out what composers would have expected in different periods, and to apply your knowledge to your own playing or singing, that these Performer's Guides have been written.

In fact, until the early twentieth century the idea of 'period style' hardly existed. When music of the seventeenth or eighteenth centuries was revived it was usually treated, by editors and performers, as if it belonged to the present day. But as the century went on, musicians began to realize that they could not safely assume that everything – including instruments, and ways of playing them – had simply been getting better all the time, and so that their usual performing style was bound to suit any piece of music equally well.

They began to look for ways of performing music of the past with greater regard for the composer's expectations: through the revival of instruments like the harpsichord and the lute, and the formation of chamber orchestras; through a growth in 'Urtext' editions, which showed (or claimed to show) nothing but the composer's intentions; through the detailed study of 'performance practice', the way music was interpreted at different times and in different places; and more recently through the widespread use of instruments of the same period as the music (or, more often than not, exact modern copies). In all this, recordings played a major part, opening up many neglected areas of musical history, as well as throwing new light on well-known works by demonstrating how their composers might have expected them to sound.

For a while, these developments led to a dismaying move to leave whole areas of repertoire to the specialists: to frown on any performance of Baroque music on the piano; to remove not just Bach and Handel, but even Haydn and Mozart, from the programmes of symphony orchestras. But this was hardly fair to the performers or to their audiences; and for students wishing to get to know a wide range of music, probably without any chance of access to period instruments, it made no sense at all. In any case, as specialist performers and scholars extended their researches into the more familiar territory of the nineteenth century, they discovered that here too there were performing traditions which have been lost or misunderstood. So it has become increasingly clear that all performances of music of the past can benefit from the knowledge and experience gained by the 'early music movement'.

One area which has lagged behind in this has been education. Very often, only those performers who have got as far as music college or university (and by no means all of those) have been exposed to ideas about period performance. And there have been few books presenting reliable information about the interpretation of the music of the past in a general, non-specialist way.

That is the gap we hope to fill with this series of three guides to the performance of music of different periods: the Baroque period roughly defined as from about 1600 to 1759 (the death of Handel); the Classical from 1759 (Haydn's first symphony) to 1828 (the death of Schubert); the Romantic from 1828 (the composition of Berlioz's Op. 1) to about 1914. The guides are aimed broadly at the Associated Board's own constituency of students (especially at the higher grades) and their teachers – not to mention examiners! But they are not designed as companions to specific exam syllabuses, present or future; and we hope they will be useful to all musicians, including adult amateurs and indeed professionals.

The three volumes all have the same plan. An introductory chapter sketches the historical background to the music of the period; a closing chapter discusses sources and editions. The writers of these, all leading experts in their fields, have taken distinctly different approaches to their tasks, so that the three volumes together offer an introduction to different ways of treating music history and musicology.

In between, each volume has an important general chapter on how the music on the page would have been interpreted by performers at the time, followed by a series of more specialized chapters devoted to keyboard, string and wind instruments and singing. All these are written by musicians who have not only scholarly expertise but also practical experience of performing, often at the highest level. One important point which emerges from these chapters is that different kinds of musicians have always learned from each other. We hope you will read all the chapters, not just those devoted to your own speciality; and also that you will gain enlightenment and stimulation from all the tracks on the accompanying CD.

Another important point which the contributors make many times over is that the task of the performer is not simply to give the most accurate account possible of the notes on the printed page. This is an ideal which has been in circulation only for a very few years in the later twentieth century. In general, for centuries, the performer has been expected to bring his or her own skill and taste to bear on the composer's conception – and in some periods to make a very substantial contribution. So we hope you will treat these guides not as a set of instructions telling you how to achieve a 'correct' interpretation, but as a source of the information you will need in order to give a stylish performance – a collaboration between the composer's inspiration in the past and your own imagination and fantasy in the present.

Sir Roger Norrington

Introduction

This volume is a real sign of the times. In fact, I think if you are reading it you are ahead of most other people in the musical world. Ten years ago hardly anyone had thought about taking the nineteenth century seriously as a subject for performance studies: everyone thought they simply 'knew' how to play the music. But now several books on the Romantic age are appearing, including this one. I think it's exciting.

Perhaps the whole business of nineteenth-century performance practice is going to be easier now that we are in the 2000s. In the 1900s we had the nineteenth century breathing down our necks. It was both far away (another age, another culture) and right on top of us (inherited without discussion, constantly played). Now that there is a whole century separating us from the nineteenth, it may be easier to be objective as well as excited by its romantic music. We need to break those bonds of unquestioning performance 'tradition' because so much can get out of shape and sentimental if we don't. All great nineteenth-century composers hated sentimentality.

As a conductor I tackled issues of nineteenth-century performance with the London Classical Players, having arrived by way of the seventeenth- and eighteenth-century repertoire. I wasn't sure what would happen if I took seriously all the information we garnered. But each time, with each composer, such extraordinary things emerged that we continued; you can hear what one might call the preliminary results on a series of EMI recordings from Beethoven through Schubert, Weber, Rossini, Berlioz, Mendelssohn and Schumann, to Brahms, Wagner, Bruckner and Smetana. Already we are nearing the end of our journey, interpreting the works of Tchaikovsky and Mahler, yet still we are surprised and excited by our findings.

Equally significant for me (perhaps more so) have been my parallel experiments with 'modern' orchestras. As far apart as Berlin and Vienna, New York and San Francisco, London and Paris, I have found that a tremendous number of performance ideas can be transferred easily from 'early' instruments to full-scale 'modern' ones. Although the players don't have historical instruments or background, they can achieve the same effect, and are surprisingly keen to try. String sections can be reduced in size, or the number of winds increased, to achieve the kind of balance expected by composers. Orchestras can sit as they were intended to, with violins divided across the stage and cellos and basses facing the audience. Players can learn the relevant tempos, bowing, articulation and phrasing.

The last major question remains in the air. Perhaps when this book is ten years old it may be common to hear a full symphony orchestra playing with 'pure tone', creating all the warmth and passion of nineteenth-century music without the addition of twentieth-century vibrato. Some of my regular orchestras are starting to be quite accustomed to this way of playing, and I can't tell you how beautiful and touching Wagner, Tchaikovsky or Elgar can sound like this. Both melody and harmony are enhanced, and a crucial nobility and innocence can emerge, even from tired old 'warhorse' symphonies. Classicism did not disappear overnight in 1828. Its continuing presence in the nineteenth century is something we neglect at our peril. This book will be an enormous help for you to ponder many such questions for yourselves.

Hugh Macdonald

Historical Background

Introduction

The music of the Romantic age is one of the great success stories of Western culture, since the major masterpieces of the nineteenth century – and innumerable compositions of lesser stature – are still the staple diet of our listening and performing today. Building on the extraordinary achievements of the Viennese classics – Haydn, Mozart and Beethoven – the composers who followed, from Berlioz and Schumann to Strauss and Mahler, gave the world a body of music that is passionately loved and admired, and which speaks with a strong, stirring voice to listeners of every generation. Those composers were addressing their own contemporaries, of course, and, although we feel a strong empathy for their music, we can only envy audiences of that age who were present when works such as Chopin's preludes, Berlioz's *Roméo et Juliette*, Wagner's *Ring* cycle or Brahms's symphonies were first played and first heard.

In the nineteenth century the balance between expression, language and technical means was wonderfully well adjusted. In a Schumann piano piece, for example, the composer's message is conveyed by an instrument that can truly convey it in a musical language that everyone can understand. What the composer was trying to say is not too complex or too obscure for his intended audience; the comfortable tonality of the music, with its chromatic inflections, is familiar and flexible; and the instrument was available for almost anyone to study and master.

At the same time there were incredible advances in the evolution of harmony, instruments and the public presentation of music, and there were some bitterly contended issues that cast composers into fiercely opposing groups. None of this alienated the general public; instead it drew an increasing number to participation in music and to its appreciation.

It may assist the understanding of this buoyant age if we take each of these three topics in turn – expression, language and technology – before glancing at some other striking features which shaped the century's music.

Expression

Expression is the keynote of Romantic music, since the composer's message was for the first time regarded as an essential element in a composition, more important perhaps than the workmanship or social function of the music. As with almost all developments of the time, Beethoven provided an irresistible model; and although some composers sought to minimize the personal qualities of their speech, it was widely assumed that the human drama embodied in the 'Eroica' Symphony or the spiritual explorations of the late string quartets (however hard it might be to put these meanings into words) provided a model for communication between composer and listener. The feelings generated by a Chopin ballade or a Strauss tone poem seemed to listeners to be the composer's very own feelings, valuable and unique because every composer was unique. The composer's individuality was raised to new heights by the arguments of Romantic philosophers that humanity is infinitely diverse and inherently fascinating. Everybody was free to express him- or herself in a personal way, and musicians had the precious advantage of speaking a language that was universal and unmistakably powerful. If E. T. A. Hoffmann and others were right to claim that music was the highest of the arts, then the force of musical expression opened doors to aesthetic and spiritual experiences to which no other kind of art or literature had access.

The composer with a strong personality and a strong message, like Beethoven with his call to universal brotherhood in the Ninth Symphony, could command the love and respect of enormous audiences. Intensity of feeling is a commonplace of Romantic music. Schumann's songs, or any page of a Wagner or Verdi opera, or Mahler's songs and symphonies, all testify to the power with which music conveyed the composer's joys and sufferings. The very vagueness of this message in, for example, a piano piece called 'Capriccio' was no bar to the belief that there *was* a message. If critics and audiences could not agree what a particular sonata or symphony was about, they nonetheless accepted the fact that it was about something. Tchaikovsky responded to a request to explain the content of his Fourth Symphony by inventing a narrative that probably had little to do with his original thoughts when composing the work; but at least he recognized that some such content was taken for granted, and was regarded by his audience as a help to understanding and appreciation.

This was a great age for programme music. In the earlier phases of Romantic music it did not strike anyone as naive to sing about nightingales or spring flowers, or to depict peasants dancing at harvest time. Whereas such charming descriptive pieces, not to mention more brutal evocations of siege, bloodshed and suffering, had been attempted by composers and enjoyed by audiences for over 200 years (Vivaldi's *Seasons* and J. S. Bach's Passions provide well-known examples), the new dimension in Romantic sensibility saw this through the prism of the composer's own vision. Beethoven's crisp explanation of the 'Pastoral' Symphony provides the clue: 'mehr Empfindung als Malerey', 'more feeling than painting'. Berlioz's *Symphonie fantastique* is more than a series of scenes of contemporary life: it is a personal drama, told by the central character, an artist who goes to the scaffold for murdering his unattainable beloved. We cannot fully understand Schumann's songs unless we are aware of the passion that tied him to his beloved Clara. Smetana's wonderful series of symphonic poems about his homeland, *Má vlast*, are not simply picturesque and historical images of Bohemia: they embody the resurgent national feeling that all Czechs shared at the prospect of creating an independent Czech nation with its own language and culture. Descriptive music was popular, effective and universally understood. Few questioned the assumption that it was valid as art, nor was any distinction made between the basic aesthetic of song and opera on the one hand, and textless instrumental music on the other.

The links between musical and literary expression were all the stronger since most composers also felt drawn to writing (and some to painting). With the exception of Chopin, nearly all the Romantics wrote memoirs, or criticism, or poetry, or librettos. It was assumed that the stuff of poetry and painting was within the proper domain of music, and that the reader or listener could respond to one just as he would to the other.

The one individual who dared to propose in the mid-nineteenth century that music should be concerned with its own inner logic rather than with the expression of feeling was Eduard Hanslick, a Viennese critic who had begun his career attached to the faith of Romantic expression, and who then evolved a more austere philosophy that looked forward to twentieth-century abstraction. It was a sign of things to come, even if the full reaction against Romanticism did not take hold until after World War I. The composer whom Hanslick most earnestly admired was Brahms, whose works clearly lean towards a more self-sufficient aesthetic. Brahms's long series of chamber and orchestral works, almost all in three or four movements without any descriptive titles, and all displaying the most masterly command of the composer's craft, might now be judged from an abstract standpoint, as if they bore no specific meaning or message. But to his audiences, and even to Brahms himself, the idea that this music was expressive and passionate, even descriptive, was far from unacceptable.

One of the clearest demonstrations of the Romantic faith in vivid expression is to be found in Wagner's music dramas, which placed music at the centre of an elaborate all-embracing art form. It has sometimes been argued that Wagner's music is so powerfully descriptive that the listener needs no voices and no staging to grasp its meaning and its impact. If only he had written symphonic poems for orchestra alone, this argument runs, he would have completely satisfied any listener's craving for evocative and moving music without the expense and contrivance of the theatre. It is true that the great orchestral passages in his operas, such as the Prelude to *Tristan und Isolde*, are at least the equal of any vocal scenes; and the final

Fig. 1.1. 1867 illustration of *Tristan und Isolde*, Act II, scene ii, by Michael Echter, based on the first production, 1865.

scene of that work, the *Liebestod*, is frequently played as an orchestral piece by simply omitting Isolde's line, a practice sanctioned by Wagner himself. But the impact of Wagner is nonetheless most devastating when the colossal power of his orchestra is blended with great singing, with clearly articulated poetic language, with the suggestive force of dramatic gesture, and with extravagant stage décor, which in Wagner's conception was to be elaborate and lifelike in every detail. All these elements combine to create an overwhelming artistic experience, unrivalled for its intensity and hugeness by anything before or since.

Musical language

The popularity of Romantic music is partly due to the richness of its language. The system of major and minor keys – classical tonality – had been well established for over a century, and had been brought to a peak of perfection by eighteenth-century masters such as Haydn, with his dexterous command of key and modulation within a finely balanced form. That language was greatly enriched by Mozart, who had an instinctive feeling for chromaticism, and who clearly enjoyed displaying his abundant powers in expressive music, especially in minor keys. In this domain Beethoven was surprisingly not a major pioneer, since his handling of harmony, at least, was never as adventurous as that of his contemporaries Spohr and Schubert: other musical elements provided his main source of power. The flexibility of securely tonal language with increasingly chromatic detail served composers from Chopin to Mahler, and provided a resource for shaping the structure of movements as well as for delineating expression. Liszt, Chopin and Schumann all felt their way firmly forward, as if allowing their fingers to experiment at the keyboard. Wagner learnt from all of these, putting more and more emphasis on appoggiaturas, notes that are not properly part of the harmony but which yearn to resolve upward or downward to a concord. Schumann's 'Vogel als Prophet' (see Ex. 1.1) is almost entirely based on the expressive, possibly even humorous, use of these appoggiaturas.

Ex. 1.1.
R. Schumann, *Waldscenen*, 1848–9, 'Vogel als Prophet' ('Prophet Bird'), bb. 1–4. Each appoggiatura is in fact a discord, and the longer the discord is held the more the ear accepts it as permanent. Resolution brings release of tension to the ear, but the chord itself gradually becomes acceptable in its own right.

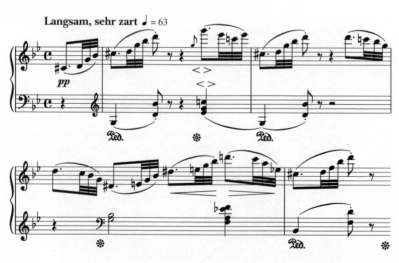

Romantic harmony made considerable use of 7th chords of various kinds, adding an extra note to the traditional three-note triad of major and minor chords. The 7th is traditionally an unstable interval requiring resolution, but it soon became tolerable to treat 7th chords and added-6th chords as consonances which do not need to be immediately resolved. The diminished 7th was a stock-in-trade for dramatic effect. The texture of Romantic music is thus often made up of four-note harmony, later extending in composers such as Ravel to five-note, six-note and seven-note harmony, without actually losing sight of the basic triad in the home key.

Although many voices were raised against the outrage that Wagner's dissonances were thought to commit, and although tonality was eventually to be undermined by the relentless extension of chromaticism, nineteenth-century audiences found late Romantic harmony both meaningful and beautiful. A deft harmonist such as Rimsky-Korsakov can enthral his listeners with magical harmonic effects, and the sensuous richness of the late music of Brahms or Verdi shows how masterly was the handling of advanced harmony within the boundaries of the tonal system. With Debussy and Skryabin the harmony becomes frankly experimental, for the chords are suspended in time without the obligation to resolve in any direction at all. The implications of this for structure and meaning were profound: so that, although more traditional composers like Saint-Saëns found Debussy's music agreeable in its effect, they were alarmed at what it might do to age-old principles of form and the inherent bond between structure and tonality.

The language of nineteenth-century music is unmistakably richer and more complex than that of earlier periods. There remains always a great value attached to melody, from Berlioz to Rachmaninoff, and the melodic gift of many of the great figures of the nineteenth century can hardly be surpassed: think of Schubert, Chopin or Tchaikovsky. Two other trends stand out in the evolution of musical language. One is the fondness for triple pulse and triple metre, and the avoidance of military-sounding 4/4 rhythms. Bellini, Chopin, Fauré, Skryabin, and many others, display a constant tendency to build accompaniment figures on triplets, especially for music of tenderness or sentiment. Triplets also lent themselves to the rubato-laden rhythmic freedom that so much late Romantic music displays, sometimes to the point where almost no pulse can be heard at all.

The other trend is towards keys further and further removed from the 'home' key of C. Whereas Mozart never used more than four flats or sharps in his key signatures, a new delight in such keys as D flat major and B major is an unmistakable feature of the music of Schubert and Chopin – to the point where the ultimately 'deep' key, G flat major, became the standard setting for music of passionate intensity, especially love duets. Chopin found the black notes of the piano more supple and expressive than the white notes; and advanced composers at the end of the century, especially the Russians, inhabited the deeper keys as a matter of course. Stravinsky's thoroughgoing dismemberment of the excesses of Romanticism was inevitably to include the restoration of bracing four-square rhythms and the composition of a Symphony in C.

Technology

The Romantic outlook that swept across Europe in the first decades of the nineteenth century coincided with a tremendous expansion in the physical and commercial potential of music, based on industrial and technological advances. The most obvious illustration of this is that most remarkable of musical inventions, the piano, which became louder, stronger, bigger, cheaper, and with better action and sweeter tone within the first few years of the century. By 1900 it had attained the stage of development which it enjoyed essentially unchanged throughout the twentieth century. (See Chapter 3 'Keyboard'.) The piano displaced the earlier fondness for the harp and guitar as domestic instruments, especially when fashioned in its upright configuration. Piano manufacturers sprang up in great numbers, and the social benefits of playing the piano were universally recognized. Composers published etudes and short character pieces in great numbers, while touring virtuosi displayed their formidable finger dexterity in the new brilliant upper octaves of the instrument, a flashy style to which even Chopin and Mendelssohn were not immune. Following Liszt's example, the idea of a complete piano recital was born. The bigger, louder pianos with their iron frames could fill larger halls and attract larger audiences. The notion that the piano could equal or emulate an orchestra was often expressed.

Orchestral instruments also enjoyed the benefits of the new technology, especially the wind. Stringed instruments changed relatively little, but the intensive application of metal keys to woodwind instruments improved intonation and agility, and new members of woodwind families, such as the cor anglais, the contrabassoon (both actually revivals from the eighteenth century) and the bass clarinet, enriched the orchestral palette. For brass instruments the introduction of valves in the 1820s had a far-reaching impact on their role in the orchestra: the rather cumbersome practice of carrying sets of crooks for trumpets and horns, which allowed the player at least to play in different keys if not on every note of the chromatic scale, was very neatly superseded by a relatively simple mechanism that brought flexibility, agility, better tuning and ultimately financial advantages to performance on brass instruments. (See Chapter 5 'Wind Instruments'.) It often seems as if the heavy brass dominates the post-Wagnerian orchestra; but it must be remembered that while the number of brass instruments in the huge orchestral works of Mahler and Strauss is incomparably higher than in a Beethoven symphony, the woodwind and strings are also vastly multiplied in number. Somehow the economics of music in the years just before World War I allowed the proliferation of huge orchestras, which seemed the right purveyors of the intense, sometimes overpowering, message of late Romantic music.

Larger orchestras needed conductors to keep them in order. It was some time before the art of conducting settled into the high-profile activity that we know today, since at the beginning of the nineteenth century it was not clear how the conductor should beat, where he should stand, which way he should face or even whether he was necessary at all. The early pioneers, such as Spohr, Mendelssohn and Berlioz, had to work these things out for

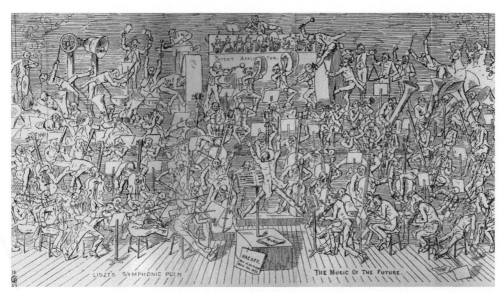

Fig. 1.2. English caricature of Liszt conducting, 1869. 'The music of the future' was the title of one of Wagner's essays, and the phrase was often applied to the progressive music of Wagner himself and his father-in-law Liszt.

themselves, though the old eighteenth-century concept of the Kapellmeister suggested that a conductor was there simply to serve the players. With Liszt on the rostrum it became apparent that the conductor was there to serve the audience too, embodying the music for the audience's sole benefit with expressive gestures and sometimes shamelessly theatrical movement.

Most of the great orchestras of Europe and North America were founded in the nineteenth century; some of them, such as the Philharmonic Society in London or the Société des Concerts (now the Orchestre de Paris), in the early years of the century. They enhanced the professional status of their musicians, and enjoyed an ever-rising standard of playing, as conservatories devoted more and more attention to specialized training. The idea of training musicians as one might train a plumber or any other artisan met with some resistance from the Russians, many of whom felt that their natural musical instincts might be sullied by contact with an alien Western culture. But it was from the conservatories of Moscow and St Petersburg that were later to come a series of great violinists and pianists: it is only necessary to cite the names of Heifetz and Horowitz to indicate the stature of the breed.

The propagation of music throughout the nineteenth century expanded enormously thanks to advances in printing and publishing. The process of lithography greatly facilitated the production of cheap music, especially choral works, songs, piano music and arrangements of operatic melodies. Publishers ceased to act solely as printers and distributors; they were becoming agents for their composers, looking out for opportunities for their music to be performed. No one matched the extraordinary achievement of Breitkopf & Härtel, the Leipzig publishers, in issuing reliable, beautifully printed editions of the great masters, nor of Röder, the Leipzig firm of music engravers who acted for publishers all over the world. Engraving music remained a highly skilled and expensive craft, but it was brought to a very high standard in this period, and its commercial viability was striking

too. The new enlarged audience for music provided a market for hosts of musical journals which appeared from every big city, many appearing weekly or twice weekly (like Schumann's famous *Neue Zeitschrift für Musik*). A quite unprecedented proportion of the population spent their money on attending concerts and operas, buying instruments and sheet music, and reading musical journals – certainly a much higher percentage than today.

Singing

Owing nothing to industrial technology, the human voice, or at least the purposes to which it was put, nevertheless underwent some significant changes. There had been great singing in the opera houses of Europe for 200 years, but there were now new schools of singing which emphasized vocal styles that best suited new styles of composition. In Italy the 'bel canto' style was the culmination of singing methods which had long been cultivated there, with sweetness, agility and elegance the prime aims. This style was perfectly adapted to the works of Rossini and Donizetti. But with French Romantic opera a new approach was required. The great new discovery concerned the tenor voice, able to reach much higher (with suit-able training) in a chest voice and with previously unheard-of lung power. From now on, operatic heroes were invariably tenors, the villains invariably baritones, and the increased realism of Verdi's operas coupled with larger, louder orchestras called for a more stentorian projection. The physical demands made on singers by Wagner's operas are legendary, and for good reason. (See Chapter 6 'Singing'.)

The nineteenth century was a truly great age for choral singing. Almost every concert which required an orchestra also required a chorus. This enthusiasm was part of the movement towards amateur participation from which music benefited more than any other art, and it was propelled also by the philanthropic belief that choral singing was an avenue by which the uneducated masses might better themselves and occupy their evenings in an uplifting activity. There was a moral and predominantly Christian impulse behind the massed choruses that gathered for big city festivals and sang Handel, Mendelssohn and patriotic songs in huge numbers. England had a strong unbroken choral tradition going back to Handel; France had developed a taste for massed forces during the Revolution; and Germany displayed a keen enthusiasm for amateur music-making within a Lutheran social structure. The popularity of Mendelssohn, Spohr and later Dvořák in Germany and England reflects this choral vitality; in France the leading figures were Gounod and Thomas.

Popular infusions

At the opposite end of the scale, the salon, always hosted by ladies of some social standing, provided an opportunity for individual singers to display their accomplishments. The most sought-after salons would present singers of renown, often from leading opera companies, while more modest gatherings allowed guests to open up their music cases and bashfully offer a song or two by Schubert, Mendelssohn, Sullivan or Fauré. This was also a route by which songs from operettas found their way into the home, the beginnings of a popular song market that grew exponentially in the first half of the twentieth century. Indeed it is fascinating to observe the gradual opening of a split between highbrow and lowbrow music. Mozart and Schubert were not too proud to write dance music, but neither Berlioz nor Wagner would dream of doing anything so vulgar. Both Offenbach and Sullivan were a little embarrassed by their success in the popular sphere, and aspired to write grander music to which they were less well suited; but by 1900 the popular theatre was served by composers whose only aspiration was to write popular music, and the musical comedy was born.

Meanwhile folk music, popular in a different sense, was embraced by serious musicians and elevated to a status of which it had never dreamt. The melodic richness and modal ambiguity of folksong offered a wonderful alternative to the well-worn formulae of the Classical style, so it contributed to the general devaluation of tonality at the turn of the twentieth century. It also provided admirable material for composers who were anxious to forge a national style independent of other nations, by which was usually meant the Austro-German tradition from Bach to Brahms. Nationalism added colour and variety to Romantic music, and it was indeed in conformity with Romantic ideology to defend the individuality and distinctiveness of every nation just as it had upheld the individuality of composers. We think of such countries as Russia, the Czech lands, Scandinavia and Spain as the breeding grounds of national schools – and indeed they produced music of a wonderfully distinctive colour. But national sentiment was proudly invested in German and French music also, even if their longer traditions waived the need to invent a new language. Both Wagner and Debussy felt every bit as wedded to their national origins as the Russian Five, or Grieg, or Sibelius.

The musician in society

It is often supposed that the patronage which secured Bach's position as a servant of the church, and which provided Haydn's employment for many years in the Esterházy household, came to an end with the fall of the

Bastille in 1789: but this is not so. The image of the penniless composer starving in his garret is strengthened by a reading of Berlioz's *Mémoires* or a hearing of Puccini's *La bohème*, but Romantic composers were never too proud to accept employment if it was offered. Mendelssohn's position in Leipzig was that of the traditional Kapellmeister, and Wagner was working his way through the established avenues as an opera-house musician when his foolhardy involvement in the Dresden uprising in 1849 put an end to that career (but not of course to his immense ambitions as a composer). Mahler followed that same professional course all his life. A few composers, such as Brahms, Verdi and Strauss, were successful enough to live off their earnings as composers, but most had to perform on an instrument, conduct or teach in order to provide for themselves and their families. If Bizet had not been so busy arranging and rehearsing other people's music, his rather brief list of masterpieces might have been longer. It is true that aristocratic patrons less frequently determined what music got composed; in their place the new patrons – publishers and impresarios – controlled the destinies of musicians more than anyone would wish to acknowledge.

From the vantage point of the early twenty-first century it is easy to envy the nineteenth century its achievements and its self-confident assurance about life and art. Having witnessed the alienation of composer and audience in the second half of the twentieth century, we would give much to re-establish that enlightened cultivation of music that made the latest opera, the latest symphony or the newest song a topic of conversation at any civilized dinner table. Films, sports and a raft of popular musics now compete for that attention, so it becomes harder and harder to recreate that now distant society and to grasp the assumptions and aesthetic standards that guided their taste. But to keep that era's unequalled treasure trove of music alive and to penetrate as deeply as we can into the soul of nineteenth-century music remains a precious goal to which we can all aspire.

Clive Brown

Notation and Interpretation

Introduction

For a long time there was a widespread idea that 'early music' ended with Bach and Handel, and that from Haydn and Mozart onwards we were on firm ground, with a continuous tradition to connect us with the performing practices of the Classical and Romantic eras. In recent years we have come to see the music of the Classical period in a rather different light, and this is now regarded as legitimate territory for the 'early music' movement. But for most musicians the dividing line between 'early music' and a tradition of performance with which we feel ourselves to be directly in touch has still not shifted beyond the beginning of the Romantic period. Many modern musicians assume that the scores of Brahms or Tchaikovsky, or even those of Mendelssohn or Schumann, mean more or less the same to us as they did to the composers' contemporaries. Even young professional musicians who are aware of recent advances in the study of performing practice may play a piece by Haydn or Mozart in a restrained 'Classical' manner, but perform Schumann, Grieg and Debussy as they would Shostakovich, Messiaen or Tippett.

Yet the truth is that at the beginning of the twenty-first century musical notation conveys something quite different to us from what it did to musicians of the Romantic period. This is not only because the sounds of our instruments and our manner of playing them has changed, but also because notation has come to be seen as increasingly precise in its meaning, with respect both to the notes and to the growing number of performance markings supplied by composers. Even in the early twentieth century, performers felt themselves to have much greater freedom, especially (but not only) in matters of rhythm and tempo, than we do today. To say that we now treat notation literally would be going too far, but we certainly treat it in a much more strictly literal manner than earlier musicians would have done. Severe critical eyebrows would be raised at a modern performer who played or sang distinctly different rhythms from those written by the composer, who interpolated grace notes for the sake of a portamento, who introduced pronounced rubato where none was indicated, or who, in keyboard playing, did not synchronize the right and left hands. Yet all these things would have seemed quite normal, acceptable, or even praiseworthy, to musicians of the Romantic period.

Our current attitudes towards notation result to a large extent from two unrelated phenomena, one intellectual and the other mechanical.

The first of these phenomena had its roots deep in nineteenth-century thinking about greatness in art. Musicians and writers, especially in

Germany, developed the idea that performers had an absolute duty to realize the composer's intentions as scrupulously as possible: as Wagner put it in 1841, in performing a composer's music the executant should 'add nothing to it nor take anything away; he is to be *your second self*'. Influenced by such ideas, a new breed of performers began to emerge. They saw their highest calling not in displaying their virtuosity in an individualistic manner, but in subordinating themselves entirely to the composer's intentions. One of the earliest of this new type of virtuoso was Brahms's great friend the violinist Joseph Joachim. As a youth Joachim had been advised by Mendelssohn that 'a true artist should play only the best'; and, in reference to music by great composers, that 'it is inartistic, nay barbaric, to alter anything they have ever written, even by a single note'. Taken at face value, such advice seems to suggest the kind of approach that is the rule nowadays; but, as a mass of evidence shows, that was not quite how nineteenth-century musicians interpreted it. It is certainly true that the general trend throughout the Romantic period was for performers to stick more and more closely to the instructions contained in the score, but it was not until the mid-twentieth century that fidelity to the composer's text was interpreted as slavish adherence to the literal meaning of the musical notation.

The second important phenomenon was the invention and development of sound recording. At first, methods of recording were primitive and restrictive, and the impact on people's approach to performance was slight. But, particularly after the introduction of electric recording in the late 1920s, when recordings rather than live performances gradually became the means by which most people got to know musical compositions, performers became increasingly self-conscious about what they were doing. Once you could listen to the same performance as many times as you liked, even the slightest deviation from what was written in the score became much more obvious, and a potential ground for criticism. By the second half of the century, people seem to have wanted recordings to be clean and clinical renditions of the notation, with interpretation confined to the most discreet and delicate nuances of accentuation, dynamics and phrasing. This is quite understandable, for strikingly individual performances can begin to sound mannered if heard time and again without variation.

Editions – text and performance

During the second half of the twentieth century, performers became increasingly accustomed to playing from 'Urtext' editions. These editions have the advantage of providing a musical text that corresponds as closely as the editor can make it to the composer's authorized version; anything that is not thought to have stemmed directly from the composer is clearly differentiated as 'editorial'. Thus you can be sure that if, for instance, a trill is shown without a turn, that is what the most reliable sources contain. But in the case of a trill without a turn, you still have to ask yourself: 'was it intended to be played without a turn, or did the composer simply assume that the performer would know it needed one?' Some, but not all, Urtext editions will provide answers to such questions, reflecting the editor's understanding of the composer's practice. The kind of performing edition that originated during the second half of the nineteenth century and remained the norm for much of the twentieth century would have supplied an answer, which probably reflected the editor's own practice. For much Romantic music the older practical editions, often edited by leading musicians of the period, can contain fascinating and very useful information about the performing practices of the time, including such things as accents, dynamics, phrasing, ornamentation, fingering and so on. More recent editions, say mid-twentieth-century editions of mid-nineteenth-century music, may present a misleading picture of the practice of the composer's contemporaries. But, however good the edition (and for more on this see Chapter 7 'Sources and Editions'), there will always be much that is necessary to perform the music convincingly which is not adequately conveyed by the notation.

Accents, dynamics, articulation and phrasing

When you study the rudiments of music, one of the first things you learn is that each bar of music contains strong and weak beats, and that these are arranged according to strict patterns, which are specific to the various metres (4/4, 3/4, 6/8, etc.). This teaching about so-called metrical accent was expounded by eighteenth-century theorists, and has been an element of basic theory teaching ever since. However, at the same time many musicians cautioned performers against taking such theories too literally, for there were other kinds of accent that were more important and often overrode the metrical accent. For instance, many early Romantic writers stressed that it would be mistaken always to make the first beat of a bar stronger than the second, even though the composer might not have indicated any off-beat accents. In the 1830s G. W. Fink wrote: 'A too symmetrical and scrupulously regular mechanical beat introduces a stiffness into the performance that equates with crudeness'. A couple of decades later Liszt condemned 'mechanical, fragmented up and down playing, tied to the bar-line, which is still the rule in many cases'. And in the last quarter of the century the theorist Hugo Riemann substantially rejected the idea of metric accent, even in relation to the performance of earlier music: he considered that phrasing could be better described in terms of crescendo and diminuendo.

Phrasing accents and expressive accents

The most important of the kinds of accent that predominated over metrical accent were those which marked the phrase structure of the music, and those which were vital to the expression (they were given a variety of names by different theorists). Fink observed that, as a rule, 'the metrical accents should not be applied anything like so sharply and strongly' as the accents that clarified phrasing. These phrasing accents were always related to the structure of the melody and its relationship with harmonic movement; they normally marked the beginning of the musical phrase and its subdivisions. Sometimes such accentuation was indicated by unusual beaming, by slurs, or by accent signs, but for the most part it remained unmarked. Even during the later Romantic era, when many composers supplied their music with numerous performance instructions, these kinds of accent were largely left to the performer's experience or instinct. It is therefore still vital for the modern performer to understand how the composer expected the music to be phrased, and to apply the appropriate accents sensitively – together with the appropriate dynamic shading which, as Riemann recognized, is a vital but often unmarked component of effective phrasing.

Expressive accents were essential to the emotional content and character of the piece. They made the music 'speak' to the listener, and were thus often referred to as 'oratorical' or 'rhetorical' accents. These accents could occur on any beat, according to the shape of the melody, the intensity of the harmony, or the explicit instructions of the composer. In music from the early part of the Romantic period you can expect to find that the composer has at least marked the most important of these accents, but there may well be other notes which also require a degree of accent to bring the character or feeling of the music to life. Such notes may invite accentuation for a number of reasons, of which the most common are dissonant or chromatic harmony, pitch (a particularly high or low note within the phrase) and length (a longer note among short ones, often involving a syncopation). Hummel, in his *Ausführlich theoretisch-practische Anweisung zum Piano-forte Spiel* (*A Complete Theoretical and Practical Course of Instructions on the Art of Playing the Piano-Forte*) of 1828, provided a series of annotated examples indicating the application of the accents, unmarked by the composer, which were necessary to 'render our discourse impressive, and the meaning [of the music] intelligible to the hearer'. He employed two symbols: + for a 'slight degree of emphasis' and ∧ for a 'much stronger emphasis', as shown in Ex. 2.1.

Some later Romantic composers, particularly in the German tradition of Liszt and Wagner, supplied very detailed markings of all kinds, while others, such as Brahms, left much more to be decided by the performer. Brahms, in fact, was very wary of providing too many instructions; he regarded them as a necessary evil when a work was totally unknown to the performers, but felt that, once musicians were familiar with the piece, superfluous instructions were more likely to constrict their freedom of expression than to aid it. The relative scarcity of markings in some later Romantic music certainly does not mean that it should be played less expressively than music with many markings. And even in the music of the most fastidious composers, many of the subtler aspects of accentuation, especially those concerned with phrase structure and expressive nuance, were still the responsibility of the performer. The ability to go beyond the composer's notation in this respect was considered to be one of the most significant hallmarks of a fine performer.

Dynamics

At the beginning of the Romantic era it is rare to find dynamics softer than *pp* or louder than *ff*. Schumann and Liszt, however, began to mark extremes with *ppp* or *fff*, and Tchaikovsky sometimes used *pppp* or *ffff*. An obvious conclusion from this is that the difference between Mendelssohn's *pp* and *ff* was greater than that between Tchaikovsky's. In the music of composers

who used fewer dynamic markings, therefore, you may wish sometimes to make *pp* very soft and sometimes extremely soft, depending on the musical context. However, you may also like to bear in mind that the nineteenth century was a period of great change in the design of many instruments. The instruments of the early Romantic period were generally softer than those of the late Romantic, which were closer to our modern instruments. (See the separate chapters 'Keyboard', 'Strings' and 'Wind Instruments'.) You should also be aware that some nineteenth-century composers used what at first sight look like dynamic markings as accents: see the section 'Accent and articulation markings' below.

Ex. 2.1. J. N. Hummel, *Ausführlich theoretisch-practische Anweisung zum Piano-forte Spiel* (1828), part 3, p. 56.

Articulation

Articulation, in the sense of varying degrees of staccato execution, was regarded as important for characterizing musical phrases or passages. As a means of marking the end of a musical phrase, it played a crucial role in punctuating the musical language and making its meaning comprehensible to the listener.

Earlier composers rarely bothered to specify articulation except where it was essential to the character of the music, and their only clear distinction was between staccato, portato and legato (indicated either by verbal instructions or by staccato marks and/or slurs). In Romantic music, too, it is sometimes uncertain whether there is any intentional difference between notes with staccato marks and notes without any marking at all, for staccato marks were still often used in mixed passages of slurred and separate notes merely to clarify which notes were not to be slurred. A number of twentieth-century musicians pointed out that in such circumstances staccato dots might not indicate a genuine staccato execution. Nevertheless, Romantic composers increasingly provided detailed information about where and how they wanted articulation in their music. Many of them began to make a clear distinction between staccato dots and staccato strokes (indicating, among other things, different degrees of separation), and a number of signs, such as ∸ or ⊤ and ‒ , as well as a range of accent/articulation markings combined with slurs, were adopted.

Slurs on their own could indicate the articulation of musical phrases as well as legato. There was a view, maintained by many musicians throughout the nineteenth century, that under certain circumstances the last note under a slur should be shortened and followed by a rest. But it is often difficult to be sure when the composer might have intended a slur to have that meaning. More frequently a slur would have implications of phrasing, and would require accentuation at the beginning and diminuendo at the end. With all these markings, though, you have to be aware that different composers used them in slightly, or sometimes radically, different ways. What is more, they sometimes mean different things in music for different instruments. Letters exchanged between Brahms (who was primarily a pianist) and his violinist friend Joachim clearly show how the same signs could convey quite different things to pianists and violinists.

Accent and articulation markings

The functions of accent and articulation are often combined in the same marking. These markings were intended to differentiate various degrees and types of accent (gentle, sharp, heavy, sustained, diminishing or agogic, i.e. created by timing) and articulation (more or less). The following paragraphs give a general indication of their range of meanings in Romantic music, but if you want to understand what they meant to any particular composer you will need to consult more specialized literature. You will also have to study the ways in which these markings are used in other music by the same composer.

f **or** *ff* Though these seem to be strictly dynamic markings, Classical composers had often used them to indicate accent, and some early Romantic composers, for instance Schumann, also used them quite frequently in this sense. It seems likely that the intention was to obtain a strong but not necessarily sharp accent.

fp This will sometimes mean literally a decrease from *forte* to *piano*, either abruptly or gradually (this can only be determined from the context). In mid-nineteenth-century music, however, it may often mean the same as *sfp* (or *fzp*). This is particularly likely in the music of Mendelssohn, and in Schumann's music up to about 1850.

sf **(*sforzando, sforzato*), *fz* (*forzando, forzato*)** There is no difference between *sf* and *fz*. Some composers (e.g. Mendelssohn, Schumann, Liszt, Wagner, Berlioz, Brahms) preferred *sf*, others (e.g. Schubert, Chopin,

Dvořák) *fz*. Many composers seem to have employed this normally as a weighty accent, while some also used it in *piano* contexts as a gentler one.

rf, rfz (rinforzando, rinforzato) This could indicate either an accent or a rapid (usually powerful) crescendo. Liszt often used it (generally written as *rinf.* or *rinforz.*) in the latter sense. Brahms may have intended it as a slighter accent than *sf*.

> This is the most commonly used accent sign in Romantic music. It will always indicate an accent that dies away. Sometimes it seems to mean the same as *sf*, and some composers, such as Verdi, preferred it to that marking. A number of late nineteenth-century composers, for instance Brahms, sometimes used a long diminuendo 'hairpin' to indicate an accent.

∧ This accent sign was not widely adopted until the mid-nineteenth century. Its relationship with > is unclear, though from its shape it suggests an accent that is more sustained, without significant diminuendo. Many composers, such as Schumann, used both accents frequently. Some writers, especially in the mid-nineteenth century, saw ∧ as a slighter accent than *sf*. In the later Romantic period, it seems to have been regarded more as a very strong accent. Bruckner and Dvořák used ∧ on successive notes in string parts as the equivalent of repeated down-bows in a *fortissimo* context (Ex. 2.2). An example of Dvořák's use of this combination occurs in the first movement of the String Quartet Op. 106, where, in the first edition score, he marked a succession of minims with both ∧ and down-bow markings.

Ex. 2.2. A. Bruckner, Third Symphony, third version, 1887–9, first movement, extract from autograph score. The ∧ signs in the wind parts indicate a series of strong accents; they are used together with down-bow signs in the string parts, indicating the equivalence of the two markings. In addition, it can be seen that Bruckner originally wrote ∧ signs in the first and second violin parts before changing them to down-bows.

— The horizontal line, either alone or in combination with a dot $\doteq$ or $\bar{\cdot}$, also came into general usage from about the middle of the nineteenth century. Normally it seems to have indicated a weighty but not sharp execution, probably less accented than > or ∧. When combined with the dot it also indicated separation, but less than the staccato mark. Even without the dot it often appears to imply a slight separation. Some writers, however, suggested that notes marked with horizontal lines should be sustained for their full value. When horizontal lines were used on a succession of notes under a slur, they generally implied slight weight and infinitesimal separation. This style of performance was called portato. The biggest source of confusion here is between ⌢··· and ⌢−−−. Both occur very frequently in nineteenth-century music for all kinds of instruments and occasionally also for voices. The lines under slurs can generally be relied upon to indicate portato; dots under slurs could sometimes mean precisely the same thing, but at other times they could mean short and sharply detached staccato or *spiccato*. This is partly a question of technique on different instruments. Violinists, for whom the slurs were essentially bowing marks, had employed the notation of dots under slurs since the eighteenth century, both to indicate a sharply detached execution, and to mean a portato bow stroke. In the nineteenth century, lines under slurs were adopted partly to prevent this confusion. But some composers who were primarily pianists, for instance Brahms, saw no need for the distinction and often marked portato with dots under slurs.

<> This sign had its origin in the old *messa di voce*, a swell usually accompanied by vibrato, which was applied to long sustained notes. Classical and Romantic composers used it as an accent sign over short notes. It was even used in piano music where no swell of the note is possible. It implied a specially expressive accent, perhaps involving a degree of lingering (agogic). In much nineteenth-century string music it will have been seen as an invitation to apply a vibrato.

· | ▾ Staccato marks primarily indicated articulation, but could also imply accent. Although the three marks may suggest three different kinds of staccato, there were in reality never more than two, since the wedge (▾) was used as a publisher's equivalent of the handwritten stroke. Some composers, in fact, used only a single form of staccato mark, and distinctions in early printed editions often resulted from misreading autographs or from simple caprice on the part of publishers. However, many Romantic composers including Wagner, Brahms and Dvořák used staccato dots and staccato strokes (wedges) with specific meanings. During the second half of the nineteenth century, printed editions are generally reliable about showing these marks as the composer wanted, since the proofs were normally corrected and improved by composers themselves. But we cannot always be sure precisely what the different forms of staccato mark were intended to convey to the performer. The stroke usually meant a more accented attack and a shorter duration than the dot. But there are exceptions to this; in French practice, for instance, the stroke seems often to have meant a shorter and lighter staccato than the dot, while in German practice it could be stronger and longer than the dot.

But there were also distinctions between the way these two marks were used for particular instruments. In string music they might indicate specific kinds of bowing (*martelé, sautillé, spiccato*, etc.); but different musicians would have used them in different senses.

In reality the music of the period requires far more gradations of staccato than even the most careful composer could indicate, and it is ultimately the performer's responsibility to match the style of staccato to the musical context.

Combined accent and articulation marks

The intention behind the combination of accent and staccato marks is usually fairly clear, in that it means both accent and separation. But what kind of accent and what degree of separation? There is no easy answer. This kind of notation may perhaps best be described as 'impressionistic'. It is an instruction to give a special character to the note or notes in question, but the precise manner in which this should be achieved is very much a matter for the performer's instinct.

The slur

The slur has a number of functions in nineteenth-century music. Its most basic meaning is simply legato. In string playing, of course, it will commonly have the specialized meaning that the notes under the slur are to be played in a single bow stroke; at the same time, though, a succession of slurs in string playing need not necessarily suggest a break of any kind between them, or an accent at the beginning of each new slur. The bow changes are unavoidable, but the intention will often be a continuous legato with dynamic nuances within the slurs as required; conversely, very long slurs might have to be taken in several bows without the change of bow being obvious. A similar situation may occur in wind music, though composers would often use slurs that were longer than could be executed in a single breath, leaving it to the player to decide where to breathe. Sometimes, however, especially in keyboard playing, the slur may have been intended to indicate accent at the beginning and articulation at the end; this was particularly true of slurs over two or three notes, but many nineteenth-century musicians felt that it was also applicable to longer slurs in keyboard playing.

Some late Romantic musicians began to favour longer slurs that were more explicitly tied to phrasing, and much earlier music appeared in edited versions where the slurring was altered to show what the editors believed to have been the composer's real intentions. In 1898, for instance, Karl Klindworth wrote in the preface to his new, and soon widely used, Novello edition of Mendelssohn's *Lieder ohne Worte* (*Songs without Words*):

> The new phrasing slurs are intended to preserve the pianist from the error of rendering the melody according to the strict rules of pianoforte playing, which would require that in every group of slurred notes the first is to be accented and the last slightly shortened in value, thus dividing it from the following group. (Ex. 2.3, overleaf)

old edition

present edition

Ex. 2.3.
F. Mendelssohn,
Lieder ohne Worte
Op. 38 No. 2,
1835–7, melodic line
of bb. 1–8, quoted in
the preface to the
edition by
K. Klindworth
(1898).

Klindworth, who was only twenty-one years younger than Mendelssohn, clearly did not believe that Mendelssohn really intended his slurs to be played 'according to the strict rules of pianoforte playing', for he later remarked that his new slurring was meant to show 'the manner in which Mendelssohn may have intended the melody to be played'. Brahms, as a letter to Joachim shows, certainly considered that the 'strict rules' only applied to slurred pairs, and that in other cases such treatment was 'a freedom and refinement in performance, which, to be sure, is generally appropriate'.

Ornamentation

The Romantic period witnessed enormous changes in musicians' attitudes towards ornamentation. As the idea that performers should respect the integrity of a composer's notation rapidly gained ground, elaborate extempore embellishment, which had been such a pervasive aspect of solo performance for much of the Classical period, became increasingly confined to particular genres of music. In Italian opera, at least up to Verdi, and in some kinds of solo virtuoso compositions, for instance the works of Chopin and Liszt, extemporizing additional ornamentation or modifying embellishments provided by the composer remained an accepted practice, one which is documented on early recordings. From the 1830s onwards, however, most composers wrote out ornamental figures and passages as they expected them to be played, either in normal or small-size notes.

Appoggiaturas and grace notes

Around the beginning of the Romantic period, many of the confusing notational practices which had originated when ornamentation was largely the performer's responsibility were superseded by more straightforward ones. As a rule, except in Italian opera, the kinds of appoggiatura that functioned as sustained dissonances resolving onto a consonance a tone or semitone below, or more rarely above, were no longer written in small notes, or left to be improvised by the performer; they were incorporated into the standard notation. Single small-size notes (increasingly often with a line through the tail, as in modern practice) were used almost entirely to indicate grace notes; these were intended to be performed lightly and very rapidly either on or just before the beat, depending on the composer's practice. In most German keyboard playing an 'on-beat' performance was still theoretically the rule, whereas in French keyboard practice a 'pre-beat' execution seems increasingly to have been favoured. On other instruments there were similarly conflicting traditions of performance. In practice, the problem may be illusory, for the Romantic approach to rhythmic flexibility will often have made it unclear precisely where the beat actually was, and as long as the grace notes are played lightly and rapidly they will make their proper effect.

Trills and turns

Composers no longer used the elaborate systems of ornament signs that were devised in the eighteenth century. A few standard ornaments, such as trills, turns and inverted mordents, were still indicated by signs, though these too, even sometimes trills, could be written out in full.

The trill was usually marked as *tr* , and composers sometimes indicated preparatory notes (Ex. 2.4a) and/or concluding notes (Ex. 2.4b). Where no

Ex. 2.4a   Ex. 2.4b

preparatory notes are marked, it is often difficult to know whether to start trills on the main note or from above. Beginning with Hummel in 1828, many writers of instruction books during the Romantic period stated as a matter of course that unless the composer indicated otherwise trills should start with their main note, not from above as had been common in earlier periods. Some early Romantic composers, however, seem routinely to have expected an upper-note start. These may have included Chopin and Mendelssohn. But the majority of composers, at least from the middle of the century, would have envisaged a main-note start where no alternative was indicated. In most circumstances a simple turn at the end of the trill would have been expected whether or not it was marked; where a different ending was required the composer normally made this clear in the notation. However, in solo pieces, especially of a virtuoso character, performers may have improvised more elaborate endings to trills, especially at cadences. On short notes *tr* might indicate the figures in Exx. 2.5a and b. The latter, however, was normally specified by ∿ . As a rule, this sign indicated only one repetition of the upper note and no turn at the end. A few composers used a rather similar sign to indicate vibrato.

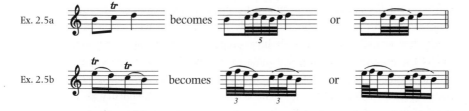

Ex. 2.5a   becomes   or

Ex. 2.5b   becomes   or

Turns were usually written as ∾ or ⌗ . They could either have been performed as four notes, beginning on the note above, or as five notes, beginning on the main note (Exx. 2.6a–c). The practices of individual composers and performers were quite varied. As with trills, the tendency during the Romantic period may have been increasingly to prefer a beginning on the main note. But many musicians would have continued to expect the traditional four-note form. The rhythm of the turn was affected by the melodic context and the tempo. It was usually meant to be performed quickly even in slow tempos, though in cantabile playing a more leisurely execution of the turn may have been characteristic of the later Romantic period. Sometimes turns marked with the normal turn sign were played as inverted turns (Ex. 2.6d); the musical context will often make it clear whether this is an option. The 'inverted turn' sign ∾ was explained by Hummel and Spohr as a normal turn, and ∾ as an inverted turn; but this seems to have had little influence on mainstream notational practice.

Improvised ornamentation

Improvised ornamentation survived only in isolated areas of Romantic music. In Italian opera it remained customary to add appoggiaturas, grace notes and more elaborate ornaments in certain circumstances, and few nineteenth-century singers would have felt any compunction about changing the ornamental flourishes provided by the composer. A certain amount of freedom in varying ornamental passages would also have been characteristic of solo instrumentalists. The opportunity for an improvised cadenza still remained in some later nineteenth-century concertos. Brahms's Violin Concerto is perhaps the most famous example, though there is no evidence of violinists actually improvising a cadenza in that work; they would almost certainly have prepared it beforehand, or played one of the published cadenzas (for instance Joachim's). For the most part, instrumentalists would not have introduced ornaments where the composer did not specify them. Some common nineteenth-century practices, however, may broadly be described as improvised ornamentation since they involved departing from the strict meaning of the composer's notation. The most important of these were vibrato, portamento and arpeggiando (in keyboard playing).

The idea of continuous vibrato as a basic aspect of tone production did not begin to emerge until towards the end of the nineteenth century. It was not widely accepted until the second decade of the twentieth century, and was not generally adopted until the 1930s. For most of the nineteenth century, vibrato was regarded as an ornament to be used sparingly in string playing, wind playing and singing to give a special character to selected notes. It was normally used on accents or to embellish an important long note in a melody. This can clearly be heard in recordings by Joachim and Adelina Patti.

Portamento, an audible slide between notes at different pitches, was seen as an important means of heightening expression in singing, string playing and even in wind playing. It grew in popularity during the late eighteenth century, and became so pervasive in the nineteenth century that leading musicians from Salieri in 1814 to Joachim in 1905 regularly cautioned against abusing it. However, as recordings show (including those of Joachim and Patti), portamento played a major part in Romantic performance. Although it went out of fashion towards the middle of the twentieth century and is generally now thought of as sentimental and tasteless, much Romantic music can benefit from a carefully calculated use of portamento.

Arpeggiation is often marked in nineteenth-century piano music with a vertical wavy line. It is clear from early recordings, however, that both arpeggiation and rhythmic dislocation (particularly playing the melody note slightly after its bass note) were very often used where the composer had not notated them. It seems in some respects to have been regarded by pianists as their substitute for portamento and vibrato, as a means of highlighting or embellishing selected notes. The use of this technique is fascinatingly in evidence in a piano roll of Schumann's 'Warum?' (from *Fantasiestücke*) made by Carl Reinecke, a pianist who was personally associated with Schumann.

Tempo

Few aspects of performance concerned nineteenth-century musicians as greatly as tempo. There was much discussion not only about establishing the right basic tempo but also about the appropriateness (or inappropriateness) of various kinds of tempo flexibility within the music. The question of varying the tempo within a movement was particularly contentious, with major composers taking strongly opposed positions.

Metronome marks and basic tempo

The invention and marketing of the metronome in the second decade of the nineteenth century provided a practical way of fixing tempo precisely. Beginning with Beethoven, major composers began to supply metronome marks for their works. But few musicians were entirely happy with the idea of giving such an exact instruction, for they realized that, as the respected theorist A. B. Marx observed in the 1830s:

> the same piece of music must sometimes be played somewhat faster, sometimes slower, according to the larger or more constricted space in which it is performed, according to the stronger or weaker forces employed, but particularly according to the decision of the moment.

And Wagner maintained that things would be in a sorry state

> if conductors and singers are to be dependent on metronome marks alone...they will hit upon the right tempo only when they begin to find a

lively sympathy with the dramatic and musical situations and when that understanding allows them to find the tempo as though it were something that did not require any further searching on their part.

After *Tannhäuser* (written between 1843 and 1845) Wagner no longer gave his works metronome marks. Mendelssohn showed considerable reluctance to use them, giving them only to a small portion of his output (he once said to Berlioz, 'anyone who cannot guess the tempo of a piece just by looking at it is a duffer'). Brahms scarcely ever employed metronome marks and forcibly expressed his distaste for them. Schumann, Berlioz, Dvořák and many other composers, however, used them regularly; in practice, though, many later performers have taken their music at quite different speeds from those specified by the composer's metronome marks.

Metronome marks are often contentious. This was true even at the time: Clara Schumann, for instance, changed a fair number of her husband's metronome marks when she issued her edition of his piano works after his death. Composers themselves sometimes revised their views or performed their music at different tempos from those which they had indicated. Elgar, for example, sometimes contradicted his own metronome marks when he made recordings of his music. Nevertheless, metronome marks certainly provide the most reliable information about the speeds composers envisaged, and may be taken as a good starting-point for understanding their intentions. Where no metronome marks are available it is very difficult to determine, except within broad limits, what the composer may have imagined, for their use of tempo terms was often highly inconsistent. Wagner's metronome marks, for example, show that, for him, an Andante in 4/4 time with quavers as its fastest notes could be anything from ♩ = 50 to ♩ = 100; and an Allegro in 2/2 (¢) with quavers as its fastest notes might range from ♩ = 69 to ♩ = 120.

Flexibility of tempo and rhythm

One respect in which nineteenth and early twentieth-century performance differed strongly from the way we tend to play Romantic music was the degree to which the tempo was modified where no change of tempo had been marked by the composer. Few if any Romantic musicians would have disagreed with Hummel's warning that in using the metronome performers should not feel 'bound to follow its equal and undeviating motion throughout the whole piece, without allowing themselves any latitude in the performance for the display of taste or feeling'. Yet there was much disagreement among Romantic musicians about where, how and to what extent such latitude might be permissible. So, if you want to perform the music of this period in an appropriate style, it is important to know where the composer stood on these matters. This is not always easy to discover; but the opposite extremes may be illustrated by the attitudes of Mendelssohn and Wagner. It was said of Mendelssohn by those who knew him that in playing 'he never himself interpolated a *ritardando*, or suffered it in anyone else', and that 'he never varied the tempo when once taken'. But the idea that Mendelssohn played with metronomic precision would be mistaken, for Joachim, who had been coached in his youth by

Mendelssohn, remarked: 'Mendelssohn, who so perfectly understood the elastic management of time as a subtle means of expression, always liked to see the uniform *tempo* of a movement preserved as a whole'. Wagner, on the other hand, was noted for introducing extreme changes of tempo within a movement. When he conducted in London in 1855, one critic remarked that 'he prefaces the entry of an important point, or the return of a theme – especially in a slow movement – by an exaggerated ritardando' and that 'he reduces the speed of an allegro – say in an overture or the first movement – fully one third, immediately on the entrance of its cantabile phrases'. It seems likely that composers such as Schumann, Dvořák and Brahms tended rather towards the Mendelssohnian position, while Wagner's approach was shared by Liszt and an increasing number of younger musicians as the century wore on. The earliest recordings indicate how much freer an attitude towards tempo flexibility of all kinds was taken   by leading musicians of the Romantic period than is customary today.

Rubato and tempo rubato

The terms 'rubato' and 'tempo rubato' are often used nowadays to describe the contrasting approaches to flexibility of tempo represented by Wagner and Mendelssohn. 'Rubato' is taken to signify the Wagnerian practice of speeding up or slowing down the basic pulse of the music in accordance with its emotional content, and your only problem in applying this to Romantic music is to know where it is appropriate and how much rubato to use. 'Tempo rubato' implies that, while keeping the basic pulse more or less stable, the performer lingers over some notes and compensates for this by hurrying others. This was very characteristic of nineteenth-century performance, and many musicians, from Spohr in 1832 to Eugène Ysaÿe in the early twentieth century, insisted that in music involving more than one player the accompaniment should remain constant while the soloist manipulated the tempo in this manner. In solo keyboard playing there was a similar lack of synchronization between the right and left hands. In practice, of course, even this kind of tempo manipulation must often have led to some flexibility of the accompaniment, thus shading over into the other kind of rubato; but, in theory, the overall tempo of a movement or section was scarcely affected. While some important later nineteenth-century composers, for instance Grieg, strongly objected to exaggerated rubato, he would not, as his own recordings demonstrate, have approved of the rather rigid manner in which music of the Romantic period is often played today. For present-day musicians, however, these techniques, involving a subtle redistribution of written note values, are difficult to master.

Rhythmic flexibility

It is fundamental to our training as classical musicians that we should adhere strictly to the note values given by the composer. We are taught that the figure ♩♪ must not be played as if it were ♩ ♪, nor should the rhythm be ♪♩. Even less acceptable would be to play a pair of equal notes as if one of them were dotted, or to make a dotted figure into two equal notes. Yet such treatment was quite normal in nineteenth-century performance. Many examples of this kind of rhythmic freedom are preserved on recordings of musicians born before or around the middle of the nineteenth century. Sometimes it was recommended for practical purposes: in singing, for instance, where an upbeat might be shortened in order to take a breath before it. Students of historical performing practice have long accepted that rhythmic alteration, including such things as *notes inégales* in eighteenth-century French music, is a characteristic of Baroque performance. It is now becoming clear that similar practices survived in a variety of forms until the early twentieth century. Often this is unconnected with the composer's notation, but it is also certain that composers as late as Grieg could notate  where they intended assimilated to triplets, as Grieg's own recording of his *Humoreske* Op. 6 No. 2 demonstrates (Ex. 2.7). The opposite effect of overdotting could also have been expected; nineteenth-century written sources recommended it as a rule in many circumstances. Wagner is reliably reported to have required this treatment of a single-dotted figure during rehearsals of *Parsifal* in 1882. Elgar allowed, or even encouraged, it when he conducted recordings of his own music. In many cases the change to the notated rhythm arose from the use of agogic accentuation, closely related to the technique of 'tempo rubato', whereby an important note was lingered over and subsequent notes were hurried to compensate. Early recordings preserve many instances of this and other modifications of the written rhythms.

Ex. 2.7. E. Grieg, *Humoreske* Op. 6 No. 2, 1865, bb. 21–7.

Conclusion

Perhaps the most important thing to remember in performing Romantic music is that the notes are merely a starting point. Despite all the detail in the score there is still enormous scope for you to respond to the music in ways that go beyond the notation. As one great late-Romantic performer, the cellist Pablo Casals, observed: 'The written note…is like a strait-jacket, while music, like life itself, is constant movement'.

Roy Howat

Keyboard

with a section on the organ by David Goode

The changing piano

You doubtless know all too well how different one piano can sound and feel from another. If you've been practising on a house or school upright piano for a week or more, then suddenly have to play on a full-sized grand piano for a concert (or even an exam), the very different sound can be quite a shock. So can the different touch and weight of the keys. Or if you've been lucky enough to have a large grand piano on which to practise, suddenly playing on an upright can be just as much of a shock: the sound that comes out doesn't seem to match the effort you're putting into the keys.

We can react to this in different ways. Some performers like to stick to one kind of piano, or even a single instrument (if they're famous enough). If we feel more inventive (or aren't rich and famous) we can adjust the way we play, for example using less weight on a less strong piano. With time and practice we can learn to adjust quickly, both by listening and by sensing through the arms and fingers how to get the best possible sound from any piano we play (unless it's a real lemon – and lemons can turn up anywhere, even in concert halls).

Most pianos we now find in houses and halls were made sometime in the twentieth century. But have you ever played a piano made around 1830? Or around 1860? If you've had a chance to try several old pianos, how does a piano made in Paris in 1830 compare with one made in Vienna or Germany around the same time, or one made in London? Anyone who has played different pianos of that period will know that not only do they feel and sound quite different from modern pianos, but also they're much more different from one another than modern pianos tend to be. Why is this?

There are numerous reasons. One is that, unlike today's, most nineteenth-century piano makers *wanted* their pianos to have their own distinct sound. The whole idea of the piano was still fairly new then, and people didn't yet have a strong fixed idea of a standard piano sound. Nor did they have recordings. There was also little established repertoire beyond Bach (perhaps) and the Viennese classics, so composers were exploring and inventing new sonorities and techniques, while piano makers were almost scrambling to keep up by developing pianos with a greater range of notes, dynamics and tone-colour. That way, makers hoped their particular piano sound would appeal to some famous virtuoso or composer, thus ensuring good publicity. This happened in the 1830s and 40s in Paris, where Chopin let it be known that his favourite was the Pleyel (he also liked the English Broadwood), while Liszt strongly endorsed the Erard. We'll shortly see how those preferences are reflected in their music.

There was another urgent reason why pianos were changing. By 1830, as Chopin, Liszt, Mendelssohn and Schumann were starting to make their names, virtuoso piano concerts (or 'recitals', a name invented by Liszt) were becoming fashionable in cities like Vienna and Paris, and a constant complaint was that the piano wasn't loud enough for a large hall. This was especially so in Austria and Germany, where pianos were still quieter than French or English ones. (That's why Beethoven, some years earlier, was so happy to be sent a piano from London by John Broadwood.) Over the next thirty or forty years various makers, from Erard in Paris to Chickering and Steinway in the USA, redesigned the piano as a louder, more robust instrument capable of filling a hall, imitating an orchestra, and, in concertos, standing up to an orchestral tutti (an effect explored in Brahms's, and even Schumann's, concertos). The piano keys, incidentally, became slightly wider.

Nineteenth-century developments

To go into these developments fully would fill a book. But, briefly, what happened is that first of all hammers were made heavier and strings thicker, to deliver more sound. Hammers also started to be covered in hard-packed felt rather than layers of leather, delivering a deeper and less 'pingy' sound. As more sound became available, composers increasingly wanted the bass to go lower and treble to go higher (see Table 3.1). All this hugely increased the tension on the piano frame – which on a modern piano can amount to twenty tons – so the old wooden frames were gradually replaced by iron ones. As the piano's insides grew and took up more space, cross-stringing was introduced, meaning that the bass strings lie at an angle across the tenor and middle strings (Fig. 3.1). Without cross-stringing, a modern concert grand would have to be about half a foot longer and its tail end a foot wider to accommodate the same string length; most uprights would have to be at least a foot higher. Perhaps even more important, cross-stringing places the bridges for the bass and tenor strings more in the middle of the soundboard, greatly increasing resonance.

Fig. 3.1. Plan view of an 1888 Steinway grand, showing cross-stringing.

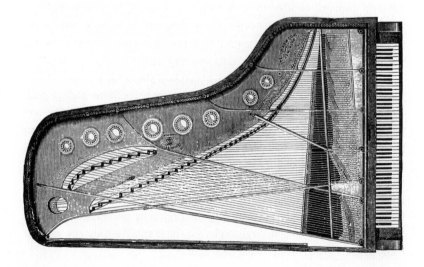

Table 3.1. The growing compass of the piano

Approximate date	Bottom note	Top note	Works that exploit (or anticipate) new range
1775	F′	f‴	Mozart (and most Haydn) sonatas and concertos and early Beethoven. Mozart's only known f#‴ for piano appears in the finale of his Sonata in D major K. 448 for two keyboards; a similar isolated f#‴ appears in the first movement of Beethoven's Sonata in E major Op. 14 No. 1
1795	F′	c″″	Haydn, Sonata in C major Hob/XVI:50; Beethoven, Sonata in C major 'Waldstein' Op. 53
1816	C′	f″″	Beethoven, Sonata in A major Op. 101, Finale (bass E′); Chopin, Etude Op. 10 No. 1
1840	C′	g″″ or a″″	Chopin, Scherzo in E major Op. 54
1870–80	A″	a″″	Brahms, Piano Concerto No. 2 (first note of piano part)
1890	A″	c‴″	Ravel, *Jeux d'eau*; Debussy, *Reflets dans l'eau*
1900s Bösendorfer	F″	c‴″	Bartók (various works); Ravel, *Jeux d'eau*, 'Une barque
(Bösendorfer Imperial	C″	c‴‴)	sur l'océan' from *Miroirs*, 'Scarbo' from *Gaspard de la nuit* and Finale of Concerto in G (by implication – see below – and probably not with Bösendorfer in mind)

These were the ranges generally available, though various pianos went beyond those at various times. For example, some Broadwoods of the 1790s cover C′–c″″; between 1822 and 1834 Erard took some pianos up as far as c‴″; and around the time of London's Great Exhibition of 1851 some French and English makers briefly covered the full seven-octave range A″–a″″ or even G″–g″″ (lower than is current even today; perhaps Ravel knew about them). Some of these larger compasses lasted only a short time because of poor tone at the extremes, or because the added string tension overstrained the frames. The treble reversion to c″″ started in the 1870s (with iron frames), but was not widespread until the mid-1890s. In the mid-1840s the young César Franck gave some dramatic demonstrations on a piano made by Jean Henri Pape with a full eight-octave range of F″ to f″″. Not until the 1990s was this compass exceeded, by the Australian maker Stuart & Sons with C″ to f‴″; a wag was heard to say that the new notes would especially appeal to offshore whales and native fruit bats.

On average, most of those developments were widely accepted by the start of the twentieth century. Often, though, they were introduced at very different times by different makers; many inventions were under patent, so adopting them could be an expensive investment. During the mid-to-late nineteenth century, therefore, different makes tended to boast different features. In the 1830s and 40s Chopin's favourite was the Pleyel, partly because its felt hammers were softer than those on the Erard and could deliver more variety and depth of singing colour (if one worked for it, as Chopin said). It also had a nicely rich but clear bass. Chopin didn't worry whether or not his sound was filling a large hall (he never cared much for giving concerts), and people just had to strain their ears to hear if necessary. Liszt, by contrast, preferred the brilliance of the sharper-toned Erard with its more incisive attack. He also preferred the Erard because of another vastly important invention, double escapement.

Double escapement

Patented in 1821 by the French Erard brothers, double escapement is now an integral part of all modern piano actions. To find out what it does, try holding down a key, then see how far you have to let it come back up before you can sound the note again. Without double escapement, the key has to come up virtually all the way, making note repetition slower, harder and less reliable. One of the earliest celebrations of double escapement is Liszt's first version (1834) of 'La Campanella' ('The Little Bell', based on the simple bell tune from the last movement of Paganini's Second Violin Concerto), which glories in fast, light repeated notes (Ex. 3.1a). Virtually unplayable on a piano without double escapement, and also well suited to the lighter, 'pingier' Erard sonority, 'La Campanella' was not only great publicity for Erard but also a stimulus to many later composers. When Liszt later rewrote the piece twice, he kept the fast repeated notes, but moved them to new contexts (Exx. 3.1b and c).

Double escapement has other benefits too. Try playing a very quiet trill, first of all from the top of the keys, and then again with your fingers virtually resting on the keybed, just letting the keys come up enough to play again. Quiet trills like this – fast or slow – occur so often in Liszt or Debussy (for example, the start of Debussy's *L'isle joyeuse*) as to imply quite a bit about how the composers themselves played. Several people who saw

Ex. 3.1. F. Liszt, 'La Campanella':
(a) version pub. 1834 as *Grande fantaisie di bravura sur La Clochette de Paganini*, bb. 297–9;
(b) version pub. 1840 in *Etudes d'exécution transcendante d'après Paganini*, bb. 54–5;
(c) version pub. 1851 in *Grandes études de Paganini*, bb. 50–52.

Debussy playing the piano were surprised that his hands always stayed on the keys, never flying up in the air (far from widespread ideas of 'musical impressionism').

Upright pianos, on which the hammers move horizontally and thus don't fall back by pure gravity, call for a modified form of escapement. Even now this is less sophisticated than on grand pianos (you can easily confirm this by experiment), and forms part of the standard 'Schwander' upright action. If you can find a single-key model of a piano action, either grand or upright – many music or piano shops have one – you can see for yourself how the double escapement works as you let the key come only part of the way back up. (Or a piano tuner can show you on your own piano, but beware of pulling the action out yourself in case you break something expensive!) The single or primary part of the escapement, incidentally, is what lets the hammer bounce back off the string even when the key is held down. That's why we don't have to bounce out of each key as we play, as we would with a cymbal or a drum: the hidden piano action does it all for us.

All these perspectives can put a new gloss on familiar-seeming music. For example, while Liszt's 'La Campanella' can still leave us breathless at the performer's skill, in the 1830s, when double escapement was little known, it would have been almost as astonishing as producing rabbits from an empty hat or making a clock go backwards. We easily overlook how much humour there is in music, sometimes because the jokes are topical to their time.

Extremes of range

Or imagine a piano concerto where the soloist starts with a note that's off the end of most pianos. That's what Brahms's Second Piano Concerto did in 1881, and the gesture may have caused quite a jolt to connoisseurs in the audience.

Other composers jumped the gun in this regard. In 1901 Ravel surprised the musical world with *Jeux d'eau*, whose climactic bar culminates in a black-note glissando from top *a#''''* (present only on the newer pianos of the time), with the left hand making as if to land on a non-existent *G#''* below the piano's compass (Ex. 3.2). Rather than have us stub our finger on the

Ex. 3.2. M. Ravel, *Jeux d'eau*, 1901, bb. 48–50.

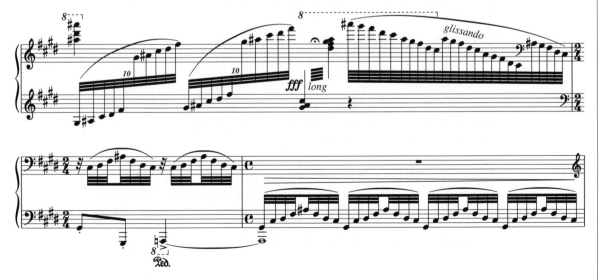

wood, Ravel mercifully makes do with the piano's lowest A'', but his manuscript shows that he originally wrote a $G\#''$ before changing it. Fortunately the sonority of most pianos, especially older Erards, lets us pull off the illusion fairly well. Four years later, in 'Une barque sur l'océan' (from *Miroirs*), Ravel went a step further again by letting that off-the-end $G\#''$ be printed in the score (bar 44), as if to say 'Come on, piano makers, where are you?' Now that one or two makes of piano have the added bass notes, we occasionally have the chance of using them, as in 'Scarbo' (from *Gaspard de la nuit*) where several of Ravel's low printed A''s and $A\#''$s suggest substitutes for the G'' and $G\#''$ below them (Exx. 3.3a and b). In the case of 'Scarbo' at least, Ravel's close colleague Lucien Garban wrote – possibly on Ravel's authority – that the lower notes should be played when possible.

(a)

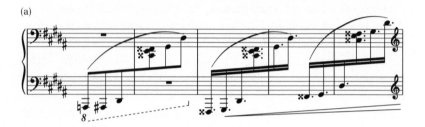

Ex. 3.3. M. Ravel, *Gaspard de la nuit*, 1908, 'Scarbo': (a) bb. 15–19; (b) bb. 395–6.

(b)

Seventy years earlier Chopin was in a similar position, having already seen the piano's compass extended during his childhood and adolescent years (see Table 3.1, p. 31). Although he never wrote explicitly outside that range, Chopin was obviously thinking beyond it, as the passages in Ex. 3.4 demonstrate (the square brackets show where the music obviously wants to go). Other examples can be seen by comparing bars 112 and 279 of the Fantasy Op. 49, and bars 307 and 315 of the Third Scherzo Op. 39. In the case of the Fantasy, so many editions of the last hundred years or more print the lower readings that even some professionals don't know they aren't by Chopin. Ravel's implied bass $G\#''$s might be seen in this context as the equivalent of Chopin's implied bass $B\flat''$s.

In the case of Ex. 3.4c, some pianos of Chopin's time – including the Pleyel he used between 1839 and 1841 and the Broadwood he played in England in 1848 – could accommodate the higher reading of bars 241–2, but for practical reasons he may have decided on printing a version that would be universally playable. Nowadays we can only guess which version of bars 241–2 he himself played on pianos that had the high g''''. For us it

Ex. 3.4. F. Chopin:
(a) Fantasy Op. 49, 1841, bb. 11–16 and 21–4;
(b) Sonata in B♭ minor Op. 35, 1837, first movement, bb. 237–41;
(c) Scherzo in E major Op. 54, 1842–3, bb. 225–7 and 241–3.

raises the quandary of 'Urtext' versus 'Urgeist' ('original text' or 'original spirit'): that is, are we being most faithful to the music by blindly following the letter or by trying to realize its probable intent? We have to make our own decisions here, from as well-informed a position as possible (for more on this, see Chapter 2 'Notation and Interpretation' and Chapter 7 'Sources and Editions'). A pragmatic comment on this comes from Debussy, whose *Les collines d'Anacapri* (Ex. 3.5) ends with a flourish reaching the same top *a#''''* as Ravel's *Jeux d'eau*; he reportedly told pianists that on older pianos without the top *a#''''* they should play *d#''''* instead (as shown on the ossia stave in Ex. 3.5).

Ex. 3.5. C. Debussy, *Préludes* Book 1, 1909–10, *Les collines d'Anacapri*, bb. 95–7.

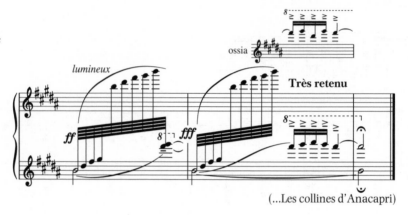

(...Les collines d'Anacapri)

Playing on modern pianos

If this is soft ground to be treading on, we cannot avoid it. Whether we like it or not, present-day instruments exist, often in response to music written earlier, and since the composers of the nineteenth and early twentieth centuries are no longer here to give us their views and advice, we have to use our own ears and intelligence. What can help us enormously is to use any opportunity of trying out music on the sorts of instrument the composers used. Playing Chopin on a well-restored Pleyel or Broadwood of the 1830s or 40s quickly makes us aware of how slow we can let a tempo become before the instrument's faster tonal decay no longer sustains the line; or how fast we can play until the action and sonority no longer articulate clearly (especially without double escapement); or how loud we can play before 'going through' the tone (making the instrument sound as if it's saying 'ouch'). Even if we may then decide that a modern piano lets us go beyond those bounds without musical damage, the experience can give us a clearer idea of the music's architecture and intrinsic colours, which we can then profitably try to maintain on whatever instrument we play. Obviously we avoid banalities such as playing Chopin quieter on a Steinway merely because an 1830s Pleyel made less sound: a Steinway played quietly is going to have a very different effect from an old Pleyel played strongly.

This applies in slightly varied ways to Schumann and Mendelssohn, whose German pianos still had a shallower touch and smaller tone than French or English ones of the time. This explains much about Mendelssohn's very nimble piano writing, since very fast figurations could originally be sounded with less finger effort than on modern pianos (such rapid strings of notes also help produce a larger sonority). Much the same goes for some of Schumann's energetically repeated rhythmic patterns, which can become very tiring (even on old pianos, it has to be said) if the shoulder, arm and wrist are not kept very free. Dangerous though generalizations are, it is probably fair to say that for the most part Mendelssohn writes for the capabilities of his pianos, whereas Schumann is often thinking sonorously beyond his.

Brahms has an interesting position here, as his career straddles a major change around the 1870s and 80s. That was when new German makes such as Bechstein and Blüthner incorporated the characteristics of English, American and French pianos, quickly seizing the lion's share of the international market and in a short time turning the German piano into something quite different. While Brahms certainly uses his piano orchestrally, some of his thicker bass textures attest to the thinner sonorities of older German pianos. And yet we know that Brahms liked the (essentially modern) Steinway: he once specifically requested one for a concert. Doubtless he always voiced his textures carefully to suit whatever instrument he was playing, but one wonders whether he sometimes even discreetly thinned out left-hand chords on instruments with a thicker bass register. In such matters nowadays, our ear and taste have to be our guide.

The shorter resonance and lighter dampers of earlier pianos, too, mean that there is often less difference between when the sustaining pedal is on and when it is off. A pedal indication in Chopin, Schumann, Liszt or Chabrier that sustains a bass note against changing harmonies above will often work on an older piano without serious smudging, while on a modern piano it may necessitate some half-pedalling or flutter-pedalling (half-pedalling means letting the dampers touch the strings momentarily; flutter-pedalling is a fast, repeated application of half-pedal). Often such subtleties of pedalling involve a compromise between not losing too much bass and not smudging too much middle and treble. As discussed below, a middle or sostenuto pedal can also sometimes help here.

It's often said (or assumed) that the twentieth-century piano, unlike the nineteenth-century one, has hardly changed at all. If this may be nearly true for the Steinway (which in the 1860s and 70s effectively set the standards for the modern piano), it applies less to some other makes, whose characteristics from around 1900 or later still have interesting things to tell us, especially when we know which makes composers liked. Although the Steinway's early admirers included Bizet, Liszt and Brahms we have no record of how Debussy or Ravel, for example, regarded it – though both of them would have known the New York Steinway in the Parisian salon of Madame de Saint-Marceau.

Ravel was known to like the Erard, whose lighter and shallower touch, combined with its fast escapement, made it ideal for fast repeated notes (as in 'Alborada del gracioso' from *Miroirs* and 'Scarbo' from *Gaspard de la nuit*), or *pianissimo* glissandi (as in 'Ondine' from *Gaspard de la nuit*). Another characteristic of the late nineteenth-century Erard, quite different from most twentieth-century pianos, is that each register has a distinct sonority of its own. This is mostly the result of straight stringing (which Erard continued to use into the early twentieth century), where the various registers correspond to different parts of the soundboard. If we play the first page of *Jeux d'eau*, or of the Menuet from Ravel's *Sonatine*, on an older Erard, an almost pungent flavour immediately emerges from the chains of left-hand minor 7ths in the tenor range. Once discovered, these can be profitably brought out on other pianos (with a bit of skill and subtlety). The woodier hammer sound of old Erards can also underline some interesting castanet effects in Ravel's 'Alborada del gracioso' (Ex. 3.6).

Ex. 3.6. M. Ravel, *Miroirs*, 1904–5, 'Alborada del gracioso', bb. 12–14.

All the same, just as with Schumann, Liszt and even Chopin, some of Ravel's more powerful 'orchestral' effects look beyond the pianos of his time. In sum, whichever instrument we play is likely to entail some compromise. For example, a Bösendorfer can supply extra bass notes for Ravel, but its heavier, deeper touch makes harder work of the light glissandos and other figurations designed for a light touch. (In fact the Bösendorfer is something of an exception among modern pianos, more closely related in its colours and timbre to the old German fortepiano, albeit with the modern deeper touch and power.)

Debussy for his part had a liking for the more sensuous touch and tone of the German Bechstein and Blüthner (making a parallel with Chopin's preference for the Pleyel). For much of his life Debussy composed on a much-loved Bechstein upright, and to this piano we can quickly ascribe one strong characteristic of his writing: the partly-filled bass octaves in pieces such as *La cathédrale engloutie* and *Reflets dans l'eau* (Exx. 3.7a and b). On a Bechstein upright these chords sometimes blend so thoroughly that we hear something more like a gong than individual notes (Debussy loved Javanese gamelan music, with its arrays of tuned gongs). Naturally we needn't conclude that Debussy's music should now be performed only on upright Bechsteins! But the effect, once experienced, can be approached on other pianos by careful voicing; for example, with firm, even fingers and the notes sounded together, as Debussy himself recommended.

 In *La cathédrale engloutie* the piano's natural sonority has more to tell us. Even on the most powerful pianos, the *fortissimo* parts of this piece are impossible to sustain in the way Debussy requests ('without hardness'), if one plays the piece at a constant crotchet tempo. In fact the message we hear from the instrument corroborates the evidence from a piano roll recorded by Debussy around 1913, in which the minims of bars 7–12 and 22–83 are played at the same speed as the crotchets around them. There is also other evidence to support this unmarked tempo equivalence, and one or two (though not all) Urtext editions now print this vital information in the musical score.

(a) **Profondément calme (Dans une brume doucement sonore)**

Ex. 3.7. C. Debussy:
(a) *Préludes* Book 1,
1909–10,
*La cathédrale
engloutie*, bb. 1–5;
(b) *Images* Series 1,
1901–5, *Reflets dans
l'eau*, bb. 89–91.

While on holiday in England in the early 1900s Debussy fell irresistibly for a Blüthner boudoir grand, which he bought and installed in his drawing room in Paris. This was the piano on which he played to visitors or worked with visiting musicians. Apparently he was especially proud of its 'aliquot system' of added sympathetic strings (which are not struck but are set above the other strings), designed to add warmth and resonance to the treble range. This is possibly a very telling point, since most pianos of that time had a shorter treble resonance than is now customary. (Steinway's 'duplex' system works similarly, with set lengths of mid-range and treble strings left free to vibrate sympathetically on the far side of the bridges.) The Blüthner also has some distinct colours, one of which emerges from the repeated low bass *A″* in the last line of Debussy's *Les sons et les parfums...* (Ex. 3.8). Again the effect, once heard, can be approached on other makes of piano. With all that, one has to remember that whatever piano Debussy was using often has to forget its identity anyway, in the course of imitating anything from a voice or an orchestra to a guitar (*La sérénade interrompue*) or even a ragtime band (*Golliwogg's Cake-Walk* or *General Lavine – eccentric*).

Sostenuto pedal

The idea of resonance prompts a question asked frequently, of how permissible it is to use the middle or 'sostenuto' pedal in music that doesn't clearly

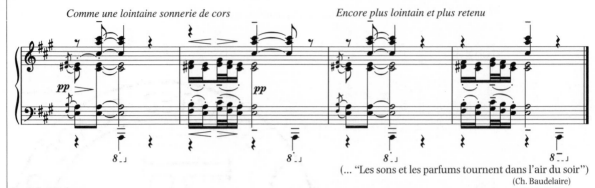

(... "Les sons et les parfums tournent dans l'air du soir")
(Ch. Baudelaire)

Ex. 3.8. C. Debussy, *Préludes* Book 1, 1909–10, *Les sons et les parfums...*, bb. 50–53.

ask for it. (Not to be confused with the muting 'practice' pedal on some uprights, the 'sostenuto' pedal, present only on some grands, allows notes to be sustained while following notes can be played staccato.) It makes a difference to know that Liszt was instrumental in the development of this device, patented by Steinway in 1874. If few composers had the device on their own domestic pianos, who can now say whether or not they were aware of it on some concert grands? Like Liszt, they may well have avoided indicating it explicitly in music which they naturally wanted to be playable on as many pianos as possible. A decision on using this pedal often depends on individual pianos and acoustics – as Debussy once said about all pedalling. (In any case, composers indicate many orchestral or vocal effects beyond what pianos can literally do – such as Brahms's famous <> swells on a single note or chord or the vocal portamento lines in bars 35–6 of Debussy's *La puerta del vino* – leaving us to work out the best way of somehow evoking or approximating to the desired effect.)

Sostenuto pedal can also help restore effects lost to us by the changes in modern pianos, for example by the more drastic efficiency of modern dampers. The main issue is really not to let any such technical device be blatant at the music's expense. Debussy's *Hommage à Rameau* (Ex. 3.9) includes one passage that cannot be literally realized without sostenuto pedal. On a piano with no sostenuto pedal we can half-pedal and try not to lose too much of the bass; fortunately it's not disastrous if the bass in Ex. 3.9 is lost a bit early. Sostenuto pedal is arguably much less useful in the *fortissimo* main theme of Debussy's *La cathédrale engloutie*, where the more watery context implies blurring of the texture (the less chromatic harmonies here also blend more agreeably), or in the Prélude of Debussy's

Ex. 3.9. C. Debussy, *Images* Series 1, 1901–5, *Hommage à Rameau*, bb. 51–2.

suite *Pour le piano* (Ex. 3.10) where, despite the tied-over bass *A'*, both feet are often spoken for already on the outer two pedals (again this can vary from piano to piano).

Ex. 3.10. C. Debussy,
Pour le piano,
1894–1901,
Prélude, bb. 16–22.

Spreading chords

The timbre and attack of an instrument also influence whether we 'roll' chords, i.e. arpeggiate them quickly, or play all the notes strictly together. On the harpsichord such spreading (albeit sometimes too fast to be obvious to listeners) is so necessary, for reasons of timbre and attack, that it is left unnotated in scores. By the nineteenth century, habits were changing along with instruments, but old habits still hung over, sometimes in exaggerated form. Chopin's famous rubato, with the hands slightly independent, was too often turned into its cheap imitation, the constant playing of left hand before right. Paderewski among others was infamous for this, and it is reported that Saint-Saëns, on hearing one of his concertos performed by Paderewski, facetiously asked the conductor afterwards which of Paderewski's hands he had decided to follow. Debussy, by contrast, is reported by friends (and can be heard on some early recordings from 1904) to have played with hands together, which is again far from any 'vague impressionism'. In that context his occasional indications for rolled chords often suggest a crisp bell-like effect rather than any weedy vagueness. (Bartók similarly used to teach his piano pupils to crush Debussy's grace notes quite crisply against the main notes, to bring out their bell-like effect.)

Conclusion

In all these matters we ultimately have to decide how much composers were thinking either within or beyond the bounds of their instruments. If Chabrier and Liszt, among many others, left broken strings and hammers after their performances, surviving accounts make it clear that they were anything but insensitive bashers: they were merely playing adventurous new music on perhaps thirty- to forty-year-old instruments, whose already obsolete designs and structure were unequal to the vigorous orchestral effects of *España* or a Hungarian Rhapsody or Mephisto Waltz. On the other hand, someone like Chopin habitually made the best of whatever instrument was available: one senses that he'd have considered string-breaking in dubious taste, and only here and there, between the lines of his scores, do we feel him really demanding something beyond his instrumental resources. At any point between those two positions there is something interesting we can learn. Far from being a dusty academic topic, an understanding of where our instruments have come from – and where they may be going – can shake a pleasing amount of dust off even the most familiar pieces in our repertoire.

The organ

The history of organ music divides more than most along national lines, perhaps because many instruments are not only unique but are also carefully matched to their buildings. Let us therefore consider each school in turn, concentrating on the German and French. English Romantic organ music, although rich both in quantity and in historical interest – for example the town-hall movement and its orchestral arrangements – is thin in real quality, with the exception of Elgar's early Organ Sonata. Nineteenth-century organ music from the periphery of Europe – Scandinavia, eastern Europe, Spain and Italy – is of specialist interest only.

The German organ of 1820 was fairly similar to that of 1720, meaning that Mendelssohn's Three Preludes and Fugues Op. 37 or Schumann's Six Fugues on B–A–C–H Op. 60 can generally be played on Baroque registrations such as the chorus pleno, on unenclosed divisions, and with a mixture of detaché and legato touch as indicated. These works reflect a revival of interest in J. S. Bach's music, led by Mendelssohn himself; yet Mendelssohn's sonatas, particularly some of the slow movements, suggest an attempt to emulate the 'sublime' style of late Beethoven. You may feel that a more Romantic approach might work here, while remembering that Mendelssohn knew neither swell-box nor pistons! Above all, Mendelssohn's music requires poise and conviction; otherwise it sounds bland.

The Romantic movement can be seen more clearly in Liszt's works. His own tribute to Bach, the Prelude and Fugue on B–A–C–H, is a dramatic piece predictably full of keyboard display. It was first played in 1856 on the new organ at Merseburg Cathedral, which, although still based on singing choruses and light reeds, possessed new richness thanks to its wide range of foundation stops. Liszt's other important organ works, the Fantasy and Fugue on 'Ad nos, ad salutarem undam' and the Variations on 'Weinen, Klagen, Sorgen, Zagen', fuse Baroque elements (chorale, fugue, chaconne) into a nineteenth-century whole.

By the time of Brahms's gravely beautiful pieces (including his last opus, the eleven Chorale Preludes) we can see a split developing: on one hand, traditional forms such as those of Bach; on the other, more adventurous creations often based on literary models. Max Reger encompassed both, composing towering fugues that build on Bach and Brahms, but also shorter, more atmospheric pieces. Today, performing his music poses two problems: much of it is very hard, although certainly well worth the effort; and it is difficult to adapt to modern organs with their bright mixtures or heavy reeds. You should use warm foundation stops whenever possible, and give this music, designed for large spaces, plenty of time to breathe. Liszt, Reger, Julius Reubke and Karg-Elert relied heavily on the Rollschweller, or 'general crescendo', but you can approximate this with a smooth build-up of general pistons (Ex. 3.11).

Ex. 3.11. M. Reger, Variations and Fugue on an Original Theme Op. 73, 1903, bb. 35–6.

By 1850 French organ music had declined from its seventeenth-century elegance into banality or sentimentality. Mainstream figures such as Berlioz, Chopin, Fauré, Debussy and Ravel wrote virtually nothing for the instrument; Saint-Saëns a few pleasant but unremarkable works. It was an organ builder, Aristide Cavaillé-Coll (1811–99), who actually began the renaissance. Alongside Ladegast, Walcker and Schulze in Germany, he gradually developed organs of a new sonority and versatility. Principals, flutes and strings were blended subtly with the rather delicate Hautbois and Trompette, now enclosed on the Récit (Ex. 3.12). The main chorus reeds were clearly descended from their eighteenth-century ancestors, and generally had even greater brilliance than English Romantic examples. They were easily operated by means of 'ventil' pedals.

Ex. 3.12. C. Franck, Three Chorales, 1890, Chorale No. 1 in E major, bb. 65–8.

RECIT Otez Voix humaine – Mettez fonds de **8**, Hautb. et Tromp.
[SWELL Remove Vox humana – Draw foundation stops, Oboe and Trumpet]

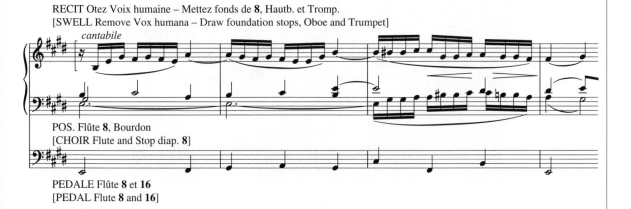

POS. Flûte **8**, Bourdon
[CHOIR Flute and Stop diap. **8**]

PEDALE Flûte **8** et **16**
[PEDAL Flute **8** and **16**]

For this type of organ, César Franck wrote his great works, culminating in the Three Chorales of 1890, in which the spirit of Bach meets the style of Liszt and Wagner. Franck was followed by Widor and Vierne, who introduced an orchestral dimension to organ music: their 'symphonies' were so-called less for their formal structure than for their size and use of the instrument. Sometimes shallow, these works are nonetheless effective, and contain several really fine movements. The French school was to blossom further in the twentieth century with the next generation of composer-organists.

How to summarize this richly diverse century of organ music? It is often said that Baroque music is modelled on speech, with its short phrases and rhetorical inflections. Romantic music is based on song, and the organist is well advised to aim constantly at making the instrument sing (note the cantabile marking in Ex. 3.12). Partly this involves a scrupulous legato, a skill we have tended to lose in our quest for Baroque articulation. But more than this, it means learning to communicate expressively with the listener – which is after all the aim of all true music-making.

Fig. 3.2. The organ at Saint-Sulpice in Paris, case by Jean-François-Thérèse Chalgrin 1779, organ by Aristide Cavaillé-Coll 1857–62. The grand appearance of this French Romantic instrument is a reflection of its rich, varied and 'symphonic' sound.

Robin Stowell

Strings

Introduction

National schools of playing have constituted the underlying foundations of nineteenth- and, to some extent, twentieth-century string performance, but they were not identifiable exclusively by any uniformity of technique and style until the establishment of national conservatories. The Paris Conservatoire, founded in 1795, was the first to cultivate a systematized approach to string teaching, encouraging, along with similar institutions in other capitals, higher technical standards and more standardized musical ideals. Many tutors for string instruments were published in the course of the nineteenth century; the names of some of their authors are still familiar today through their collections of studies, their larger compositions or their association with famous composers. (There are references to many of the tutors later in this chapter.) On the evidence of these publications, we can trace the influence of the French tradition, fostered by the Italian violinist Viotti, in Brussels (where it was continued by Vieuxtemps, Wieniawski and Ysaÿe), and further afield in Vienna, Norway and Prague. Italian string players were more individualistic, and scarcely formed a systematized 'school' in the same way, though individuals such as the violinist Paganini, the cellist Piatti and the bassists Dragonetti and Bottesini had a significant impact on the development of idiomatic playing techniques. German players, for example, among violinists, Spohr, his pupil Ferdinand David, and David's pupil Joachim, admired the Italians' technical facility, but adopted a more serious and conservative approach, deploring the exploitation of technique for commercial rather than artistic aims. However, as the century progressed, national playing styles became less well-defined, and a more homogeneous international style gradually evolved. Nevertheless, individuality was still an expected and valued component of nineteenth-century performance.

Social change and virtuoso ideals

Public concerts became an important focus for social life in the early nineteenth century, and the violin emerged as the principal instrument, alongside the piano, for virtuoso display. Violin concertos by Spohr, Bériot, Vieuxtemps and Paganini displayed numerous bravura techniques, many of which were incorporated in the more symphonic works of Mendelssohn, Brahms, Bruch, Tchaikovsky, Wieniawski and Edouard Lalo. This trend was mirrored in concertos for cello by Schumann, Dvořák and Saint-Saëns, and for bass by Dragonetti and Bottesini. Virtuosity was also nurtured in duo sonatas, character pieces and particularly opera fantasies, variations or potpourris; and composers such as Berlioz, Weber, Tchaikovsky, Wagner and Richard Strauss made dramatic technical advances in orchestral writing, especially in the lower string parts. Demands for greater volume and brilliance of sound had resulted in various modifications in instrument construction (involving the neck-setting, fingerboard, bridge, bass-bar and soundpost) towards the end of the eighteenth century, and these changes were implemented over a substantial transitional period (*c.*1760–*c.*1830).

Instruments and their accessories

The body outline of instruments of the violin family remained substantially unaltered during the Romantic era, despite attempts at 'improvement' and the introduction of new designs such as François Chanot's guitar-shaped violin, Félix Savart's trapezoid violin, Hermann Ritter's *viola alta*, Michel Woldemar's *violon-alto* and Jean-Baptiste Vuillaume's enlarged violas. Bernhard Romberg devised a cello fingerboard which was recessed under the C string to accommodate its wider vibrations; Spohr adapted this invention to the violin, but the grooved fingerboard remained neglected by most string players. The double bass was, then as now, less standardized; three-, four- and five-stringed instruments were to be found and tunings varied, but by mid-century the four-stringed bass, tuned in 4ths from E′, was the norm.

String materials changed little. The violin's upper three strings were normally of plain gut, while the G string and the G and C strings of the viola and cello were generally of gut wound with silver or silver-plated copper wire. Double bass strings were also of the latter kind or else thick gut.

Spohr's invention of the chin rest (*c.*1820), positioned initially over the tailpiece but later normally to its left (G string) side, slightly altered the appearance of the violin (and viola). Together with the shoulder pad first mentioned by Baillot in 1835, it helped to standardize the manner of holding those instruments, the resultant chin-braced grip offering players increased comfort, security and independence of left-hand finger movement as well as greater facility in shifting. The endpin, introduced by Servais in about 1850 (although Robert Crome mentions a similar device as early as *c.*1765), performed an equivalent stabilizing function for the cello. It only gradually became accepted as a standard fitting but played a significant part, in its various forms, in the development of left-hand technique and in improving tone quality.

Violinists, violists and cellists were thus encouraged to be more adventurous in shifting to the higher positions on all strings, thereby exploiting increasingly their instruments' higher ranges and cultivating greater uniformity of string timbre within phrases. Sequences were played wherever possible with matching fingerings, bowings and string changes (Ex. 4.1a), and the increased incidence of position changes on repeated notes (Ex. 4.1b) and semitone shifts facilitated achievement of the prevalent legato ideal. In cello playing, the natural, perpendicular placement of the left hand on the neck gradually gained favour over the 'oblique' position, derived from violin technique, with the thumb positioned on the C-string side of the neck and the fingers falling at a slant on the fingerboard (see Fig. 4.1). The thumb became a vital playing member and, as with the violin and viola, a prime agent in a more refined shifting mechanism. The more stable

(a) [Allegro]

4th pos. . . . . . . ⌐ 3rd pos. ⌐ 2nd pos. 1st pos. ⌐

(b) [Moderato]

p *tiré*

Ex. 4.1. L. Spohr, *Violinschule* (1832): (a) sequence with similar fingerings, bowings and string changes, p. 113; (b) shifts on repeated notes, p. 176.

methods of holding these instruments also allowed freer use of expressive devices such as vibrato and portamento.

Portamento

Portamenti, involving perceptible slides when shifting, were regarded as indispensable constituents of expressive execution of the longer, less meticulous phrases and legato character of much nineteenth-century music. Normally employed slowly in slurred bowing and mostly ascending and sliding with the beginning finger – subsequently described by Carl Flesch as B-portamenti (Ex. 4.2a) – they assisted in both articulating melodic shape and emphasizing structurally important notes. Baillot and Habeneck recommend their tasteful introduction, especially in slow movements or when sustained melodies ascend (with crescendo) or descend (with diminuendo), as in Ex. 4.3.

Fig. 4.1. J. Gunn, *The Theory and Practice of Fingering on the Violoncello*, second edition (1815), showing a 'perpendicular' left-hand position resembling modern technique (left) and an 'oblique' left-hand position (right) considered by Gunn to be antiquated yet employed by numerous early nineteenth-century cellists. The middle figure shows extended position.

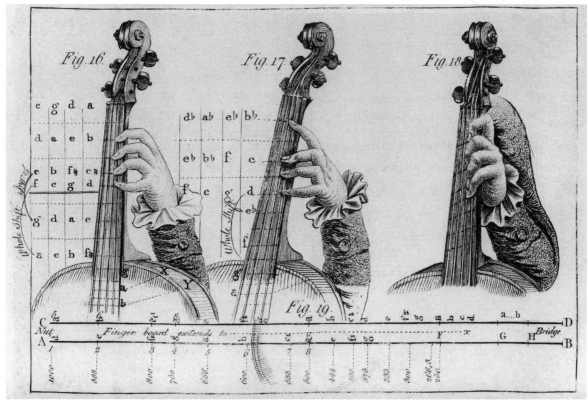

Ex. 4.2. C. Flesch, *Die Kunst des Violin-Spiels*, vol. 1 (1923), p. 30:
(a) B-portamento;
(b) L-portamento.

Ex. 4.3. F. Habeneck, *Méthode théorique et pratique de violon* (c.1840), p. 103. Portamento, ascending with crescendo and descending with diminuendo.

Involving imaginative fingerings and appropriate variation of speed and intensity of the 'slide', portamenti became so prevalent and prominent among late nineteenth-century players such as Joachim that succeeding generations reacted strongly against them. In their *Violinschule* of 1902–5, Joachim and Moser base their discussion of portamento on that of Spohr, who insists on the B-portamento for large intervals, largely rejects the L-portamento (Ex. 4.2b, in which the last finger slides from an intermediate note) and aims to avoid any 'unpleasant howling' or audible intermediate notes. He considers portamenti as necessary requirements of 'fine style or delivery' and illustrates their use, ascending and descending (Ex. 4.4).

Ex. 4.4. L. Spohr, *Violinschule*, p. 209. Portamento, ascending and descending.

In his writing on the subject, Bériot (1858) describes three distinct styles of portamento: *vif* (fast); *doux* (gentle); and *traîné* (dragged) for a plaintive expression. Vaslin (1884) largely rejects portamento on the cello, but Dotzauer (1832), Kummer (1839) and Romberg (1840) recommend it, and Max Bohrer applies it especially extravagantly in his Third Cello Concerto (Ex. 4.5).

Ex. 4.5. M. Bohrer, Cello Concerto No. 3 Op. 10, Rondo, bb. 67–9.

Interestingly, portamento was by no means confined to solo or chamber music playing. It was used by many nineteenth-century orchestral musicians, though its introduction was haphazard and lacked the unanimity of application and style fostered in present-day practice.

Vibrato

A. C. Deacon's view in the first edition of Grove's Dictionary (1878–89) that 'the Vibrato and Tremolo are almost equally reprehensible as mannerisms' was reflected in most nineteenth-century performances and publications. Introduced at various speeds and intensities, vibrato was added only sparingly as a colouring to articulate melodic shape, enhance expressive notes within phrases or assist in cantabile playing. Baillot confines its introduction to occasional 'long notes or when the same note is repeated', while Spohr provides useful examples of its restrained ornamental application (Ex. 4.6). Joachim and Moser recognized 'the steady tone as the ruling one' and used vibrato only when expressively appropriate. Similar restrictions were prescribed in cello treatises by Dotzauer and Romberg, while some writers, notably Duport (1806), neglect vibrato completely. Warnings from numerous late nineteenth-century writers against excessive use of vibrato, notably by Vaslin, suggest that its use was on the increase as a regular colouring which could be intensified or removed for special effect. This is confirmed by the evidence of early recordings.

Ex. 4.6. L. Spohr, *Violinschule*, p. 228. Annotated incidence of vibrato, including appropriate speed of vibrato oscillation. The signs above bb. 5 and 8 indicate a vibrato which starts slowly and accelerates along with the annotated crescendo, and that above b. 6 indicates the application of a consistently fast vibrato oscillation of the relevant finger.

Bows

The Tourte-model bow, developed around 1785, gained universal approbation only slowly. While French makers such as Persois, Eury, Henry and Peccatte regarded it as their ideal, others persisted for some years with pre-Tourte designs. An assortment of bows (and a diverse vocabulary of bow strokes and bowing styles) thus co-existed in the early nineteenth century, before the Tourte model's potential for fulfilling the prevailing aesthetic and expressive aims was fully recognized. Later modifications to Tourte's design included the addition of the underslide to the frog; the indentation of the frog's channel and track in the bow; the combination of rear and upper heel plates into one right-angled metal part; and a tendency for sticks to become more heavily wooded, with a consequent increase in weight, in order to achieve greater sonority. The slimmer head and different camber of Voirin's design, which offered a lighter yet stronger stick, achieved some popularity around 1850 with makers such as Lamy, the Thomassins and Bazin, but Tourte's design eventually regained its supremacy.

In the late nineteenth century a different 'German' type of bass bow, named after Simandl, co-existed with the Tourte-model (nicknamed 'French' or 'Bottesini') bow, and in some areas, notably Britain, the convex 'Dragonetti' bow. This was a hybrid of cello and viol models with hatchet head and concave camber, but with marked separation of hair and stick at the frog.

Bow grips

Fig. 4.2. L. Spohr, *Violinschule*. The manner of holding the Tourte-model bow.

The most common bow grip of the period involved placing the thumb at the frog, though some players positioned the thumb a short distance from it, even with Tourte bows. Contrary to some theorists' views, the thumb was evidently slightly bent and was commonly placed opposite the second finger or between the second and third fingers; separation of the index finger from the others on the stick was not advised (Fig. 4.2). In violin and viola playing, the elbow took up a position closer to the body than formerly, necessitating a characteristically high, supple wrist position, especially when bowing at the heel (Fig. 4.3). Although the upper arm was generally used in long strokes (but less so than today), especially in cello playing, the fingers and wrist were the focal members in cantabile bowing. Finger flexibility and variation of hand-weight and finger-pressure on the stick proved vital when making smooth bow-changes, especially at the heel.

Fig. 4.3. L. Spohr, *Violinschule*. The high, supple wrist position when bowing at the heel.

The usual 'overhand' grip was employed with 'French' bass bows, but the 'Simandl' and 'Dragonetti' types were grasped endways, meat-saw fashion, the palm enclosing the frog, the fourth finger below the hair/slide and the thumb resting on the stick (above) and acting as pressure agent, as is still common in Germany and Austria.

Bow strokes

The advent of the Tourte bow shifted the emphasis away from the articulated strokes, subtle nuances and delayed attack of most mid-eighteenth-century models to a more sonorous cantabile style, in keeping with the more expansive melodic lines of Romantic composers. It allowed for the judicious use of longer slur groupings as well as the development of a wide variety of articulations involving specific combinations of slurred and separate bows, introduced according to the prevailing character of the music in order to provide variety and so sustain the listener's interest. Some strokes, notably the 'Viotti' (Ex. 4.7) and 'Kreutzer' bowings (Ex. 4.8), were named after famous violinists who are believed either to have first employed them or to have used them regularly.

'Viotti' bowing

Ex. 4.7. L. Spohr, *Violinschule*, p. 136. 'Viotti' bowing, executed in the upper third of the bow. The first note of each pair is played softly with little bow, while the second requires a longer stroke and considerable degree of pressure for the *forte* 'accent'.

'Kreutzer' bowing

Ex. 4.8. L. Spohr, *Violinschule*, p. 137. 'Kreutzer' bowing. Alternate pairs of notes are played staccato and legato, the second note of the staccato pair being played *forzando*.

The Tourte bow also offered the capability of a more or less immediate attack, *sforzando* effects and accented bowings (e.g. *saccadé* and *fouetté*). *Martelé* bowing, comprising short, forceful 'hammered' strokes on the string at the point, was well documented in the nineteenth-century treatises; slurred staccato, essentially a succession of *martelé* strokes in one up- or down-bow, was also commonly prescribed.

Various 'bounding' strokes in which the hair leaves the string (e.g. *spiccato*, *sautillé* and *ricochet*) were gradually introduced. Nevertheless, as David's editions of Beethoven's violin sonatas verify, nineteenth-century string players tended to play more on the string than we do nowadays. The lifted stroke, generally used in the eighteenth century in the execution of dotted figures such as in Ex. 4.9a, was often displaced by an on-string stroke, two notes per bow, in which the movement of the bow was checked momentarily (usually for no more than a demisemiquaver's duration) within each pair, and the second note sounded through gentle wrist movement (Ex. 4.9b).

The 'rule of down-bow', which required notes of rhythmic stress (for example, the first note of each bar or various accented beats of the bar) to be played with the stronger down-bow and the unaccented beats with the weaker up-bow, was still valid in emphasizing the hierarchy of the bar. But

(a)

(b)

Ex. 4.9. (a) The lifted stroke, commonly employed with pre-Tourte bows, contrasted with (b) the 'tucked-in' stroke, generally used with Tourte-model bows.

it was no longer as rigidly enforced, because almost equal weight could be applied to the down- and up-strokes with the Tourte-model bow, and the longer phrases and increasingly more complex bowings prescribed in nine-teenth-century music made its dogmatic application impractical.

Like their predecessors, nineteenth-century composers were not always consistent in their prescriptions regarding slurring and articulation. Such inconsistencies have been regarded by some as examples of hasty and inac-curate notation, while others have assumed that such contrasting slurring was intentional and aimed at achieving variety or a feeling of spontaneity in performance. This variety also extended to orchestral performance. Except for isolated examples such as Habeneck's Paris Conservatoire students' orchestra, the uniform bowings of today's orchestras were not part of general nineteenth-century practice. This was especially the case in Britain, as even early recordings of, for example, the orchestra of the Royal Albert Hall or the Hallé Orchestra will verify. Players in Vienna, Berlin, Barcelona and New York are reported to have adopted a more disciplined approach to such matters towards the end of the nineteenth century.

Performance directions

The progressively more intensive and sophisticated use of performance directions (tempo indications, dynamics, articulations, etc.) bears witness to nineteenth-century composers' attempts to exercise more detailed control of interpretation. However, the respective meanings of staccato dots and strokes have been the focus of much debate. Many theorists main-tain that the stroke implies a shorter articulation than the dot, irrespective of the prescribed dynamics; others claim that there was no universal agree-ment about which indication required the shorter staccato. Still others have argued that strokes implied a stronger and longer interpretation than dots, while Spohr regarded the degree of separation as a matter of taste, not notation. Nevertheless, there was a growing tendency among nine-teenth-century string players for strokes to be associated with the more powerful, accented bowings such as *martelé* (normally near the point, but sometimes near the heel) or a short and weighty *détaché*, while dots often, though not exclusively, implied lighter bowings such as *sautillé* or *spiccato*, as described in David's *Violinschule* (1863).

Multiple stopping

The less yielding qualities of the Tourte bow led to different approaches to multiple stopping. Three strings could be played simultaneously, by pressing on the middle string, near the fingerboard, in a down-bow at the frog (but only in *forte*); or a three-note chord could be spread. Four-note chords also continued to be spread, but Spohr introduced the modern prac-tice of breaking a four-note chord upwards in twos, where the lower two notes (played together before the beat) are only of short duration and the upper two notes (played together on the beat) are sustained for their full length. A down-bow was normally employed, even for consecutive chords, but arpeggiation of chordal progressions was less common than formerly. Open strings were generally sounded (where possible) for greater sonority in multiple stopping.

The harp

Sébastien Erard's development (*c.*1810) of the double-action mechanism, based on the already established 'fork' principle, overcame the restrictions which had affected the single-action harp's capacity for modulation in the eighteenth century. Using C flat as its open key, the double-action harp initially comprised forty-three strings (*E'* to *e''''*) of gut and wire-covered silk (often now replaced by nylon), and seven adjustable pedals, each with two further positions for sharpening each string respectively by one or two semitones. The new instrument possessed the flexibility to cope with the greater harmonic and tonal demands of nineteenth-century composers, as well as allowing the execution of harmonics, *glissés*, enharmonic unisons produced by the pedals, and the chordal glissandos exploited by performers such as Elias Parish Alvars and described by pedagogues such as Theódore Labarre (1844) and Carlos Salzedo (1921). Its design has been used, with very few modifications, by makers nowadays; two American companies, Lyon & Healy and Wurlitzer, have manufactured the most robust modern models, which combine strength, efficiency, tonal improvements, mechanical precision and a slightly increased range (forty-six or forty-seven strings ranging from *D'* or *C'* to *g''''*). Despite the influence of Parish Alvars, much of the Romantic solo harp repertoire is effectively salon music and was performed largely by enthusiastic amateurs. But the instrument played an important role in the orchestra, particularly in opera and ballet and often in pairs, as well as in chamber music, with the French school predominant by the end of the nineteenth century.

The guitar

The transition from the five- to the six-course guitar was accomplished in the late eighteenth century by luthiers such as José Pagés, Louis Panormo and René Lacôte, preference being given to flat-backed models. Developments also included raising the bridge, addition of a saddle and pins to fasten the strings, substitution of an open soundhole for the rose, and modification of the instrument's proportions to align the twelfth fret with the junction of body and neck. Separate fingerboards were introduced, at first flush with the table but later raised slightly above it, while machine heads replaced wooden pegs, and fixed frets (of ivory or ebony, and later metal) were substituted for gut. Pagés and Josef Benedid also introduced an internal system of fan-strutting to strengthen the lower half of the table and cross-strutting above the soundhole, allowing the addition of higher tension strings and a consequently greater tonal palette.

Fundamental playing techniques changed little at the beginning of the century. The instrument was supported in various ways, including a strap round the player's neck and Dionysio Aguado's special invention, the 'tripodion' (a three-legged stand designed to support the guitar in the optimum playing position instead of resting it on the left thigh). The right hand was still normally supported on the table and right-hand finger-movement was restricted principally to the thumb and first two fingers. *Tirando* technique, in which the playing finger is raised after plucking the string, was most commonly employed; *apoyando*, in which the finger brushes the string and rests on the string below, was scarcely mentioned or applied. Opinion was divided regarding the role of the fingernails in sound-production, Aguado favouring their use but Fernando Sor opposing it. The left-hand thumb was sometimes employed to stop notes on the lowest string, a technique made possible by the narrower fingerboard.

The early nineteenth-century guitar was further developed by the Spaniard Antonio de Torres Jurado, who enlarged and standardized the instrument's size and form, and established the playing length of the strings at 65 cm. His development of the modern bridge and his use of a system of seven struts radiating from below the soundhole, with two further struts lying tangentially below the 'fan', were also significant, restoring the guitar's viability as a concert instrument and galvanizing further experiments in design.

Torres's work sparked off various technical developments, notably by Francisco Tárrega, who freed the right hand from its supported position and firmly established the use of *apoyando*, rejecting the use of the fingernails. Successors such as Miguel Llobet and Andrés Segovia developed a right-hand technique which employed the fingertips and fingernails to yield a wide range of tone-colour and volume. Such advances in instrument making and technique prompted an enlargement of the guitar repertoire from its staple fare of transcriptions (of, for example, music for lute, vihuela, keyboard or even bowed instruments) to original works in various genres (including concertos, etudes and chamber music), textures and styles.

Playing Romantic music today

Even though treatises and other historical sources provide solid founda-tions for our investigations into nineteenth-century styles of string performance, the information they offer is often incomplete and can some-times mislead; and it is well acknowledged that every player inevitably adds to a performance his or her own personality, style and musical perceptions, many of which may be of current rather than historical validity. Nevertheless, it is always healthy for performers to be aware of the various instrumental differences, techniques and interpretative ideals that governed performance at the time the music was written.

Nineteenth-century writers insisted that performers should communi-cate faithfully the composer's ideals, aim to move their audiences, and model their execution on that of the best singers. In attempting to emulate nineteenth-century performance on string instruments as closely as possible, you should consider how your instrument and its accessories relate to 'period' models and how you might attempt, through detailed study of the relevant principal source materials, experimentation and some educated guesswork, to fulfil the technical and aesthetic ideals of the period.

In so doing, you may call into question the continuous and often fairly slow vibrato practised nowadays on most bowed string instruments, as well as the infrequent use of portamento, or the common employment of accented and off-the-string bow strokes. Additionally, you should bear in mind the general interpretative issues discussed in Chapter 2 'Notation and Interpretation': notably the predominant nineteenth-century trend towards legato performance; the debatable value of metronome markings;

rhythmic alteration and alignment; subtleties associated with accentuation and rhetorical delivery; the merits of 'tempo rubato', tempo modification and the dislocation of melody and accompaniment in characterizing extended compositions and signalling changes of mood or tension; the varied interpretation of ornaments and the incidence of extempore ornamentation; and the overall tendency for Romantic interpretations to be volatile, flexible, vigorously projected in broad outline, but relatively informal in rhythmic detail.

You may then find yourself fighting against those requirements of precision, control, literalness, clarity of rhythmic detail and evenness of expression encouraged nowadays (perhaps principally because of the demands of the recording industry) in favour of a freer, more spontaneous and inherently musical product, inspired by considerations of historical style and governed by that ubiquitous, elusive quality of good taste.

Trevor Herbert

Wind Instruments

Introduction

My intention in this chapter is to guide you through some of the main issues about performance practice in the Romantic period, and to explain how they can be of interest to you. Much of what I have to say is applicable to all wind instruments, because, though woodwind and brass are different instrument families, they shared some styles and influences during the Romantic period. But equally there are features that are particular to individual instruments or groups of instruments, so I have also included shorter specialized sections. I hope that you will read the whole of this chapter, not only the bits that seem most relevant to your instrument, because one of the secrets of learning about performance in the past is to get a sense of the whole picture and not just your corner of it.

Anyone who has been lucky enough to play on a genuine nineteenth-century instrument, or a high-quality reproduction, will have been surprised and impressed by the experience. Such instruments often feel very different from the one you normally play. They have a different weight; they fit into the hands differently; you often feel that blowing one feels physically different – the breath leaving your lips seems to meet a different level of resistance from what you are used to – and of course the sound, the voice of the instrument, is unexpectedly different. It is as if the instrument is saying something about the sound world it came from.

Many professional wind players liken the process of playing period instruments to an experiment. They look at historical evidence and attempt to understand it, and try things out to see how well they work: they try different tempos, expression marks and shades of dynamics to find out what composers really meant by their instructions.

But not everyone is lucky enough to be able to play period instruments. You may play an instrument made in the second half of the twentieth century, and do so either with modern piano accompaniment, or in a band, orchestra or ensemble in which everyone – like you – plays modern instruments. What, you may ask, is the point of finding out about nineteenth-century performance practice if you are playing on a modern instrument? I think the answer is that it helps us understand and perform the music better. In any case, playing a period instrument is only part of the process of discovering how wind players performed in the nineteenth century. There are other equally important things to look for, and these other things are as accessible to you as they are to anyone.

In the nineteenth century, ways of playing were much less standardized than they are today. So when you prepare your music for performance it is worth thinking about the things which might have been important when the music was first performed. One such consideration is the context, the circumstances in which the music was originally written and performed. Just as a jazz band player today plays in a different way to an orchestral player, so there were differences between the playing styles of, say, military band players, salon players and orchestral players. Playing styles often varied from country to country, and different designs of wind instruments were popular in some places and not others. The way the instruments were used – the performing techniques of the players – influenced composers, who sometimes wrote wind music with a particular player or type of player in mind. Many composers often wrote in a way that suited the techniques of the performers they knew.

Much of the evidence of what Romantic composers understood to be the special qualities of each wind instrument – the 'idiom' of the instrument – is found in the most obvious place: the music itself. The figurations, the choice of phrasing, the expression marks and dynamics reveal much about the character of the instrument for which the piece is written. These markings are messages not just from the composers but from the performers too, because (as is the case today) composers often consulted with performers, and some composers of wind music were players themselves. The trick is to understand all the meanings contained in these messages. Sometimes the written notes and words do not convey the entire meaning of a piece. Imagine everything that is missed from a joke when we merely read it, without hearing it told by a really funny comedian. Your task is to use this chapter as a way of getting further into the music and catching its original spirit. Remember that this guide is meant to be practical; it is not merely about music history. As you read you should try to think about *your* playing style. Indeed, it would be good if you were to apply some of the ideas I discuss to pieces which you are studying at the moment.

Inventions and designs

The design of most wind instruments changed considerably in the nineteenth century. Woodwind instruments had additional mechanisms by the beginning of the Romantic period, but continued to be developed and refined. Brass instruments changed most of all, the main development being the invention and application of valves. I do not intend to provide a comprehensive description of wind instruments here, but it is worth outlining some of the more important general changes that took place. You will see that this section prompts you to think of how these developments affected sound and playing techniques.

Brass instruments

Valves were introduced as a means of helping players to play all the notes in the chromatic scale. The first valve-instruments were made in the second decade of the nineteenth century. At that time, horn players used hand-stopping and changes of crook (extra lengths of tubing which determined the fundamental pitch) as standard techniques. Trumpet players also used these techniques, but some leading players (particularly in England) played slide trumpets. Keyed trumpets were in use at the start of the nineteenth

Fig. 5.1. Keyed bugles. These were used in bands, while more traditional designs of trumpet were used in orchestras. Players of them mastered very advanced techniques.

century, but these appear to have been made in very small numbers. Keyed bugles, however, were much more common, and they were made in several different sizes.

The problem with the early valve-instruments (originally they had only two valves) was that while – in theory at least – the valves offered the potential for complete chromaticism, the instruments didn't always work very well: different combinations of valves produced poor intonation and unevenness of tone. It was not until the 1840s that consistently reliable valve-instruments were designed and manufactured in large quantities. The most important centres for invention and manufacture were France, Belgium, England and Germany (and later the United States). The newer instruments didn't just have better designs; they benefited from an improved manufacturing process. Good-quality metal was easier to obtain, and though a lot of cheap, shoddy instruments were made, the better instruments were of a consistently high standard. Valves were also applied to trombones, and many valve trombones were in circulation. In Italy, in fact, valve trombones were much more common than slide trombones (this is why there are so many fast chromatic runs in some Italian works of the period); but the slide trombone continued to be used, and it was seen as a quite different instrument, with a different character from the valved variety.

The important thing to grasp about the advent of valve instruments is not just that the instruments looked and sounded different; it is that they changed the way that players played. In addition to providing a simpler means of playing the full chromatic scale, valves gave players facilities which were probably not even thought of by the early inventors. Most brass-instrument valves are worked by pressing and releasing the three most agile fingers of the right hand (horn players use the left hand). Valves thus provided a means for legato playing, and made possible a new type of

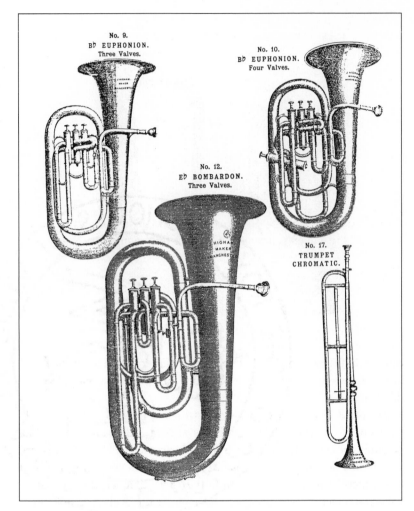

virtuosity. If you play valve brass music of this period, it is important to remember that a piece may have been written to show off valve technique.

Woodwind instruments

By the time the Romantic period began, some of the most important developments in the design of woodwind instruments had taken place, but further changes occurred throughout the century. Many of these changes accommodated the fact that instrumental sound was generally becoming more powerful. They also influenced tone-colour and technique. The achievement of fully chromatic instruments, with air-tight mechanisms and reasonably consistent timbre across the range, meant that makers could now concentrate on developing instruments with bore shapes and hole sizes which would produce an improved tone, and with more effective key mechanisms. I will touch on some of the details when I deal with individual instruments later. In the meantime, it is worth remembering why the main developments – the Boehm system on the flute, the 'Boehm' oboe (actually produced by Buffet in 1844), the clarinet perfected by Klosé and Buffet in the early 1840s, and the somewhat later modifications to the bassoon by Heckel – took place at all: they were aimed at providing players with a larger array of sound colours, and with mechanisms which (as with valve brass instruments) made it possible for performers to achieve smoother phrasing and a higher degree of virtuosity.

Old instruments versus new inventions

One of the fundamental misunderstandings about nineteenth-century performance practice is that new instruments – the newest mechanized woodwinds and valved brass – immediately replaced older-style instruments. Think of it: it is 1845 and you are a player in the prime of your professional career. Someone comes to you with a new type of instrument, and tries to persuade you to abandon your trusted instrument and take up this new contraption. What reason would you have to do so? The new instrument would cost a lot of money, and it would involve you learning a new set of techniques. It stands to reason that many – perhaps most – players stayed with the instruments which they knew. Also, many composers were fairly old-fashioned. Brahms, for example, was relatively conservative in his approach, and his brass music often called on old-fashioned techniques for playing. On the other hand, composers such as Berlioz, Wagner and Elgar were keen to use the facilities which modern instruments provided. All this tends to emphasize the need for you to think about the history and context of each piece you are performing.

Where wind players performed

Many solo works were written for each of the main woodwind and brass instruments during the Romantic period. Comparatively few are by really great composers. However, important figures did write extensively for woodwind and brass in their orchestral music, with the result that solo playing developed as much in the context of the symphony and opera orchestra as in the chamber and solo repertoire. This is an important consideration for solo performers, because some of the greatest wind players were not soloists but orchestral musicians.

The modern symphony orchestra became established in this period. It was larger and had a wider spectrum of instruments than the Classical orchestra, and while nineteenth-century orchestral music contains many wind solos, blocks of sound from brass and woodwind sections were also exploited. There was a tendency for the timbres of the brass section to be heavier, and woodwind colours to be clearer and more brilliant. But this was in comparison with the eighteenth century. Compared with today, nineteenth-century orchestral instruments had lighter sounds with clearer, more focused articulation. In the later twentieth century a preference for more mellow and expansive sonorities developed.

However, most brass and wind players of the nineteenth century did not play in orchestras; they played in bands, either military or brass. Today such bands are sometimes regarded as being of a lower status than orchestras, but this was a little less true in the Romantic period. Some military band players were among the most respected professional soloists, and many of the solos published in the period were not for professionals at all, but for technically accomplished members of amateur brass bands. Band players – amateurs and professionals – often played a different repertoire from orchestral players, and they adopted a rather different approach: they were less concerned with fine detail than they were with the display of sparkling virtuosity or with emphasized lyricism. Also, there were many salon players who played in a lighter style associated with chamber music.

There was another category of wind music-making which gained in importance in the nineteenth century, that of chamber music for wind ensembles – in various unstandardized combinations. Many composers wrote chamber music including woodwind or brass instruments which was intended to be performed in the orchestral, rather than band, style. Ensemble repertoire is especially good to play, not just because it is so enjoyable, but also because the writing is usually suited so precisely to the idiom of each instrument. So, to get the most from ensemble playing, you must read and listen to the music very carefully. Listen to the way that timbres are matched or contrasted, and try to reach a consensus with the other players about articulations, phrasings and expression marks.

Let me give just one example of how knowing the context or intention of a piece of music can influence the way you perform it. Look at the triplets in Exx. 5.1a and b. (The variations were written for trumpet, but I hope you will be able to make sense of my illustration even if you play a different instrument.) Should the triplets be single-tongued or triple-tongued? How fast should these passages be played? I am sure that you know that the speed of a piece often determines the type of tonguing you use. However, the point here is that it does not especially matter in Ex. 5.1a, since many players would have played the phrase as fast as it could be single-tongued, so that each individual semiquaver speaks clearly. The triplets in Ex. 5.1b, on the other hand, must be triple-tongued because this variation was written to demonstrate precisely this skill. There is no instruction in the music which says 'triple-tongue this section', but we know from the grouping of so many triplets and from the nature of the piece that this is what the composer intended. It follows that the tempo of this passage is determined by the speed at which the appropriate articulation can be used.

Ex. 5.1.
(a) C. Kreutzer, Variations in G major for trumpet and orchestra, 1837;
(b) F. D. Weber, Variations in F major for trumpet and orchestra, written between 1827 and 1840.

Vibrato, tone-colour, rubato

There were different approaches to vibrato in different countries and at different times in the nineteenth century, but the most common practice seems to have been that it was not used continuously and indiscriminately as part of a player's 'normal' tone-colour, but sparingly as an expressive device. The way that early twentieth-century players performed probably reflects practices that had prevailed for much of the previous century, and early twentieth-century gramophone recordings show that woodwind and brass players did not have a perpetual vibrato. But there is other evidence too. French instruction manuals from the period warn that only the very best players know how to use vibrato effectively, without making it seem coarse and tasteless ('There should be no vibrato...used by inferior instrumentalists'). And this view seems to be in keeping with what was said on the subject in an early edition of Grove's Dictionary, at the turn of the century:

> when, as is too often the case, it degenerates into a mannerism the effect is either painful, ridiculous, or nauseous, entirely opposed to good taste and common sense, and to be severely reprehended in all students whether in vocal or instrumental music.

A difference between then and now is that military and brass bands in the nineteenth century played at a much sharper pitch than they do today. Indeed, until 1966 British brass bands played instruments pitched almost a semitone higher than modern standard pitch. It is therefore worth keeping in mind when playing nineteenth-century pieces that the sound would have been brighter and clearer.

As for rubato, many younger players are reluctant to use it, because they are taught (quite properly) to play accurate rhythms and maintain tempos metronomically. However, early recordings show that soloists used rubato freely, and it seems to enhance the style. It is worth experimenting to see whether rubato can be introduced tastefully into works from this period. (See Chapter 2 'Notation and Interpretation'.)

The instruments in more detail

The flute

In 1832 and 1847 respectively Boehm designed two flutes which influenced several other makers. The latter model forms the basis for the flute of today, but in the nineteenth century no single design was used universally. The new instruments were metal and cylindrical, and used a sophisticated key system without finger-holes. The tone-holes were large, and a redesigned mouth-hole provided a comfortable support for the embouchure, which made it possible to produce a clear sound without the 'hissing' of breath escaping between the mouth and mouthpiece. The metal construction and the altogether larger dimensions of the holes and tubing gave the instrument the potential for a greater volume.

Metal flutes were not used everywhere, however. By the start of the twentieth century they were adopted in France, Belgium and Italy and in several American orchestras, but wooden flutes continued to be used in Germany,

Britain and eastern Europe. The sound of wooden flutes was mellower; writers of the time acknowledged that metal was clearer, but said that it tended towards shrillness when played loudly. There is some evidence of vibrato being employed, but rarely continuously: rather, it was used for added expression at important moments in a piece. Nineteenth-century flute treatises deal at some length with articulations and the need for expressive playing, especially in respect of rubato. This suggests that you should study expression marks in the music of this period in fine detail. However, Paul Taffanel (1844–1908), who taught at the Paris Conservatoire and was among the greatest players of his time, was said to loathe 'cheap sentimen-tality, excessive expression, endless vibrato or shaking of tone, in a word all cheap tricks which are as undignified as they are unmusical'.

The oboe

By the beginning of the twentieth century two different types of oboes and schools of playing existed, and this division probably represented differ-ences in taste which had applied for much of the Romantic period. France, Britain and the United States followed the schools of playing based on instruments developed in France by the Triébert family, while the German/Viennese instruments with wider bells continued a tradition based on a much older model developed by Josef Sellner. Indeed Sellner's book *Theoretisch-praktische Oboeschule*, published in 1825, was still widely used in the early twentieth century. The French instruments took narrower reeds, while the wider reeds used on the German-type instruments tended to produce what was sometimes described as a trumpet-like sound. Richard Strauss believed that the sound produced by the German instrument was too thick.

Because of the lyrical qualities of the oboe, the mastery of a good breathing technique is essential, and it is interesting to note that several great oboe players have also been fine singers. A valuable insight into the nineteenth century is found in the writings of Leon Goossens, the great English player. When he started playing, early in the twentieth century, he found the prevailing style to be 'wooden' with very little vibrato. He regarded Beethoven, Berlioz and Wagner as the nineteenth-century composers who, in their respective generations, best understood the idiom of the instrument.

The clarinet

In contrast to other woodwind players, most clarinettists in the late nine-teenth century seem to have used broadly similar styles of playing. This resulted from the general adoption of the German 'reed below' technique, and the wide influence of French instruction manuals. The clarinet was seen as a particularly romantic and expressive instrument, and this may explain why, in comparison with other wind instruments, it has more solo works by major composers of the period.

The different sizes of clarinet were not employed merely because of the keys in which they were pitched, but also because of their distinctive tone-colours. There is little evidence of vibrato being used, and most early recordings of clarinet players show them to be using a warm but straight

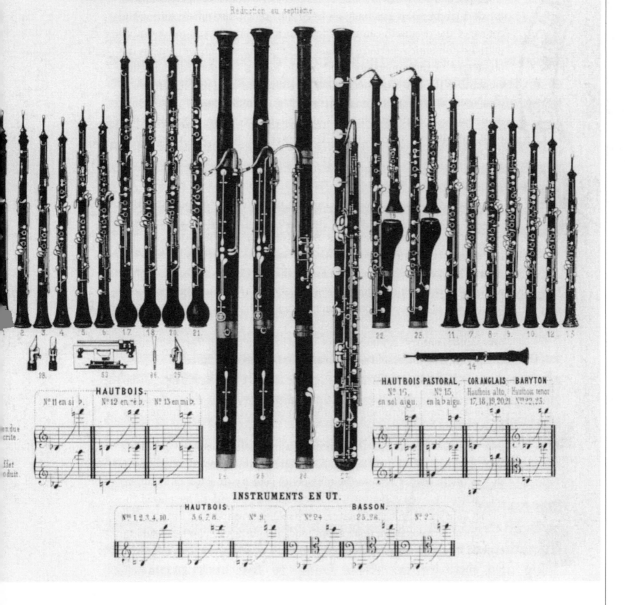

sound. An early twentieth-century American clarinettist likened clarinet vibrato to 'sugar on ice cream'. One of the features of modern clarinet playing which seems to have been less valued in the Romantic period is the consistent use of smooth articulation across the range of the instrument. Many early instruction books recommend that players listen to the different articulations used by singers. This suggests that clarinettists employed much more varied articulations than are used today.

The bassoon

Two types of bassoon were used in the Romantic period: the French and the newer German (or Heckel) bassoon. The French instrument was played with a more freely vibrating reed, and it was quieter but with a brighter and more brilliant tone-colour than the German instrument. Berlioz said that the sound of the bassoons he knew lacked 'brilliance, sonority and nobility'; perhaps to produce the weight of sound which he felt was lacking, he employed four bassoons in many of his orchestral works. In many countries the German bassoon gradually replaced the French instrument during the course of the twentieth century. The important thing for you to remember with the Romantic repertoire is that much of it was written with one or the other type of instrument in mind: music for the German bassoon often emphasizes the lower registers, while in writing for the French instrument composers would explore the higher register and make greater use of chromaticism. It is worth keeping this in mind and trying to think about the right tone-quality for each piece. Treatises of the time tend to be rich in detail about articulations, and other matters of technique.

The saxophone family

The saxophone was patented in 1846. It is important to remember that Adolphe Sax intended the saxophone to be a family of instruments, with each member having more or less the same character. By the end of the century the alto and tenor instruments were the most widely used, but several different sizes were used in French military bands, where they often replaced clarinets and almost saw off bassoons. In the Romantic period it was the use of the saxophone in military bands that was most widespread, but several composers also introduced it into orchestral music. When nineteenth-century commentators described its sound, they did so by comparing it to voices and string instruments, especially the cello.

The trumpet and cornet

Because the two instruments are today often played by the same players, many trumpet and cornet players believe that the two instruments are interchangeable, and that the techniques for playing them are, and have been, identical. Both instruments have come to share some techniques in the twentieth century, but in the nineteenth century they were fundamentally different. Most nineteenth-century trumpet players never played the cornet, and specialist cornet players were seldom trumpet players too.

The valve trumpet, an instrument made primarily of cylindrical tubing, evolved from the valveless 'natural trumpet', which continued to be used long after valves were invented. The style and technique for playing it, in the nineteenth century, were therefore much the same: a straight, brilliant sound was required, but not too heavy and loud, as well as precise articulation. In England the slide trumpet was used throughout the nineteenth century; the most common valve instrument was pitched in (low) F, with the modern B♭ trumpet being regarded as the 'high B♭ instrument'.

The cornet – sometimes called the *cornet à pistons* or the cornopean – was, on the other hand, always a valve instrument with a greater proportion of conical tubing than the trumpet. From the time when it was invented, it was perceived as a different instrument from the trumpet, with a warmer, less penetrating sound. Nineteenth-century writers refer to the occasional 'tasteful' use of vibrato by cornet players. In any event, recordings suggest that the articulation was clean and clear, and that musical phrasing was of the utmost importance.

By the mid-nineteenth century the cornet was being used as an orchestral instrument. It is worth studying orchestral cornet parts because they show the instrument in the light of three separate styles, each different from the trumpet idiom of that time. The cornet was used for its agile, virtuoso qualities (as in the Spanish Dance from Tchaikovsky's *The Nutcracker*); for its warmer, more lyrical sound (for example in the opening passage of the famous cornet solo in the Neapolitan Dance from Tchaikovsky's *Swan Lake*); or as a part of a more rounded treble-brass sonority in the larger orchestral works of composers such as Berlioz.

The saxhorns (tenor horns, baritones and euphoniums), flugelhorns and tubas

The group of instruments that became known as saxhorns was so called because the instruments are based (like the saxophone) on the inventions of the Belgian maker Adolphe Sax. In some countries the instruments are known by different names. Most saxhorns share basic design features, and the tubing from which all are made is primarily conical. For our purposes the flugelhorn can be regarded as a member of this group, even though it is technically the valved version of the keyed bugle. Instruments similar to the flugelhorn, saxhorns and tuba (sometimes called the 'bombardon') existed before Sax worked on his designs in the 1840s; however his designs were especially effective, and the instruments proved marketable to military bands and amateur players.

Nineteenth-century writings about saxhorns do not especially distinguish between one type and another as far as performance technique is concerned. There is little nineteenth-century repertoire written exclusively for them, except for some brass band solos. Saxhorn soloists often played cornet solos which in turn could have been written originally for other instruments. The playing techniques must have been similar to those associated with the cornet because cornet soloists were the most widely heard and imitated. The best players cultivated a mellow sound, sometimes with a touch of vibrato (even late nineteenth-century Salvation Army bandmasters advised against using vibrato too often), and there seems to have been an emphasis on smooth phrasing and clear articulation. Virtuosity was prized, and the dramatic effects of fast valve slurs and double- and triple-tonguing were always employed where such opportunities arose.

In the nineteenth century many of the bass parts played today on the tuba were played on other brass instruments, such as the keyed ophicleide, which had a much lighter sound than the tuba. Ophicleides were still in use up to the 1870s. In Italian opera orchestras the lowest brass part was labelled 'cimbasso', and this often signified an instrument similar to a valve bass trombone. Nineteenth-century orchestral tuba players had to balance with trombone sections which (usually) played narrow bore, softer-sounding instruments.

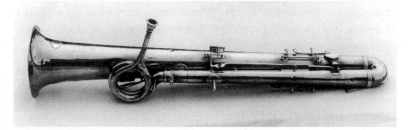

Fig. 5.4. The ophicleide was invented in 1821 by the French maker Halary. It was the bass member of the keyed bugle family. It continued to be used until well into the second half of the nineteenth century, even though valve bass instruments were available. The instrument shown here was used by Samuel Hughes, the greatest British ophicleide player. He played with the Cyfarthfa Band at Merthyr Tydfil in Wales before his distinguished career as an orchestral player, soloist and teacher in London.

The french horn

The horn was called the 'french' horn only in England; elsewhere it was known simply as 'horn', in translation. Though valves were applied to horns, many players continued to use hand horns, and some composers continued writing in a style which was as well suited to hand-stopping and the use of crooks as it was to valve instruments. As the century progressed, a new idiom was developed which included both kinds of horn, but even at the end of the century valved and valveless horns were regarded as two distinct instruments, rather than the one being an adaptation of the other. In the 1890s one commentator admitted that 'much difference of opinion exists as to the superiority of the simple hand-horn or the more modern instrument furnished with valves'. Players of modern instruments who try to capture the spirit of the more velvety nineteenth-century horn sound find that it helps to remember that the F horn was used most at the time, and they try not to neglect the F side of the double horn in favour of the B♭ side.

The trombone

Trombones in the nineteenth century were generally made from narrower-bore tubing than they are today, but German instruments had a medium to wide bore. As a general rule, the narrow bore makes for a lighter, sweeter sound than wide-bore tubing. Mouthpieces were smaller than today's, and few bass trombones had thumb-trigger attachments, even though the technology was available. The first nineteenth-century trombone virtuosos were based in Paris and Dresden. The test pieces written for the Paris Conservatoire show that florid and virtuoso playing was held in high regard, and that a wide range of articulations, lip trills and tasteful leaps over wide intervals was the order of the day. Composers and players were keen to exhibit the character of the slide trombone, to show that it had a distinctive idiom, and that the instrument was just as agile as the valve trombone. On the other hand, the great American slide trombonist Arthur

Pryor played in a style more suited to valve instruments in a brass band: his solos were little more than vehicles for his virtuosity.

Reading the music

I have given the final section this title because I think that it is the key to using some of the ideas in this chapter to make your playing more interesting and enjoyable. You should *not* try to imitate the sound of a nineteenth-century instrument on a modern one. It would be a disservice to your modern instrument, and it would almost certainly sound wrong – even ridiculous. But it is worth seeing whether some of the ideas that have come from historical research and performance can help you better understand and transmit the spirit of the music. Here are some basic tips (and you will find more on many of these subjects in other chapters of this book):

- If you have a choice, always play from a good edition, i.e. one which contains the composer's original markings.
- Find out basic information about the piece: when was it written, for what purpose, who performed it, and so on. Good editions often contain such information.
- Try to decide whether the piece was intended to be a really expressive work, or whether it was written merely to show off the technique of a performer.
- Look carefully at all the expression marks, phrasings, dynamics and tempos, and try to interpret them in a way which captures the spirit and mood of the piece. Do not over-indulge in vibrato, but experiment with rubato.
- Try to find out more about the history of the instrument you play. There are lots of good books, and the period instrument recordings which are now available reveal much about the sound world of both wind and brass instruments in the Romantic period.

David Mason

Singing

Development in vocal production

In the chapters of this guide that deal with instrumental music it is made clear that one of the most important things to remember in aiming for a stylistic, historically informed interpretation is the nature of the actual instrument. Of course, the human throat did not develop throughout the nineteenth century in the way that the lighter wooden-framed fortepiano known to Beethoven evolved into the modern iron-framed Steinway. However, it could be said that there was a parallel development in the way the voice was produced, ranging from the lighter, florid manner of the earlier years of the century (and still dominant in the 1830s) to the heavier, plainer style of Wagner, Richard Strauss and Puccini, in which the voice often has to battle with a huge orchestral accompaniment. Therefore, if we are to achieve a true nineteenth-century style we need to look at the actual vocal production. It is clear from studying singing methods and treatises that it is almost impossible to separate style and technique, as the sorts of exercises and vocalises that nineteenth-century singers practised had a direct effect on the final musical and artistic result.

The prevalent vocal style of the 1830s was what we usually refer to as 'bel canto', an Italian term meaning simply 'beautiful singing'. Definitions of the term usually refer to beauty of tone, elegance of phrasing, a perfect legato, and virtuosity in florid music. These qualities were not to be sacrificed for dramatic expression, or mere power. That is not to say that the words or the drama were not important; rather it was a question of keeping all the different elements in balance. As the century progressed, orchestras got bigger, and opera aimed for more dramatic intensity on a large scale. Consequently the bel canto ideals, as realized particularly in the operas, and songs, of Bellini, Donizetti and Rossini, were emphasized less (though they are still to be heard on many of the recordings made at the beginning of the last century) as sheer power became more important.

These changes are reflected in what is perhaps the most important source for the study of nineteenth-century singing, Manuel García's *Traité complet de l'art du chant* (*A Complete Treatise on the Art of Singing*) of 1840–47. Whereas most of the earlier treatises had stressed the importance as a training device of the *messa di voce* (that is the practice of a long crescendo–diminuendo on one note, starting with a delicate attack), García recommended the use of an altogether harder attack, activating all the ringing power of the voice from the start. This he called the *coup de glotte*, or 'stroke of the glottis'. In García's day much confusion was caused by the use of this term, and today many people take it to mean the use of a glottal plosive, where the vocal cords are held tightly together and then pushed open by the pressure of breath. It is unlikely that García would have recommended a manner of attack that is regarded by laryngologists as potentially harmful to the voice, and in a later book he made it clear that with the attack there should be no impulse of the breath. One might compare the vigorous declamation of the phrase 'Any more?' in English (or more vividly a phrase such as 'a bit of butter' pronounced in a strong Cockney accent: 'a bi' of bu'er') with 'Andiamo!' or 'Hola!' declaimed respectively by an Italian or a Spaniard, to hear the difference. As native Italian and Spanish speakers hardly ever use glottal stops, a vigorous and immediate onset can be executed without any adverse effect. It is most likely that García was advocating such an attack.

Another important vocal development described by García was the use of different timbres: the *voix claire*, the 'clear voice' of what we would think of as 'normal' singing; and the *voix sombre* or *voix sombrée*, the 'dark voice' or 'darkened voice'. The darker colours of the *voix sombrée* are a result of singing with a lower larynx. In this timbre the vowels become modified so that (Italian) 'a' approaches 'o', 'e' approaches French 'eu', 'i' approaches French 'u', and 'o' approaches Italian 'u'. Modern scientific studies have shown that this lower position of the larynx helps create a *formant*, or band of resonance, that is able to project over an orchestra. This manner of singing is now almost universal in the world's opera houses. It should be remembered, however, that in the nineteenth century the *voix sombrée* was just one of two main timbres, and would not have been used constantly. By combining the two timbres with more ringing or more veiled qualities, the singer was expected to produce an almost infinite range of colour, often with great variation during the course of a single phrase.

Types of voice

With the development of a heavier and darker vocal production, the nineteenth century saw something of an evolution of different voice-types. Not only were voices developed to produce more weight and cutting edge to cope with the larger and louder orchestras, but different vocal qualities were exploited for dramatic purposes. Thus we have the soprano heroine, the mezzo-soprano 'femme fatale' (such as Bizet's Carmen and Saint-Saëns' Delilah), and the contralto mother figure or confidante. Parallel to the soprano heroine we have the romantic tenor, the lover or hero, while the lower male voices provide some of the most dramatically and psychologically interesting roles. Especially notable are Verdi's baritone roles, which range from father figures through noblemen to villains (Germont père in *La Traviata*, Don Carlo, Iago in *Otello*). Similarly in Wagner the lower parts are usually psychologically more challenging than the tenor roles; for example Wotan, in the *Ring* cycle, is one of the greatest of all bass-baritone roles.

Different voice-types also came to be representative of different national styles. Wagner, writing in 1868, commented that earlier in the century the singing voice had been developed solely in the Italian manner. And indeed the vocalism required for Rossini, Bellini and Donizetti, with the emphasis on flexibility and florid singing, is very much based on the art of the *castrati* of the Baroque and early Classical periods. But already in the operas of

Mozart we see the beginnings of the different types of soprano, the coloratura and lyric sopranos (e.g. the Queen of the Night and Pamina in *The Magic Flute*) and the more dramatic soprano (e.g. Electra in *Idomeneo*). Later we see the emergence of the *lirico spinto*, a heavier lyric voice capable of a dramatic quality and cutting edge when required. This is the type of voice needed for many of the great roles of Italian opera, such as Leonora in Verdi's *Il Trovatore*, or Puccini's Tosca. The Germanic dramatic soprano tends to be a slightly lower-lying voice, but capable of cutting through a large orchestra in all parts of the range.

It should not be thought that these categories are cut and dried: a dramatic voice, for example, may be capable of florid singing. Maria Callas learned the part of Elvira in Bellini's *I puritani*, a role containing some hair-raising coloratura, while she was performing Wagner's Brünnhilde. Many singers move into a heavier *Fach* (category) as their voices mature. The great nineteenth-century German soprano Lilli Lehmann began her career with light coloratura roles, and progressed through almost all the different voice-types, eventually becoming a famous Brünnhilde.

The nineteenth century also saw the consolidation of the mezzo-soprano voice. What in the Classical period would have been simply one kind of soprano gradually established itself as a different voice-type. The dramatic mezzo developed as a complementary voice to the spinto or dramatic soprano; its higher range was exploited so that paradoxically there is little difference between a dramatic mezzo and a dramatic soprano. Even the distinction between soprano and contralto is not always clear, as the latter voice may sometimes develop into a dramatic soprano. However, away from the world of opera, there developed a more lyric contralto, with less emphasis on high notes, and a greater exploitation of the voice's darker colours. This is the voice for such works as Brahms's Alto Rhapsody, and the song cycles and symphonic solos of Mahler. And of course it is associated with the English repertoire, in such great works as Elgar's *The Dream of Gerontius*.

It is perhaps the tenor voice that evolved more than any other throughout the nineteenth century. During the previous century, it had been the custom to sing high notes gently; and although singers began to aim for more ringing top notes, it was usual for tenors in the first two or three decades of the nineteenth century to use a light production for high passages. Whether this would have been what we now call 'head voice' or a real falsetto is impossible to say. All this changed with Gilbert Duprez, who has been credited with singing the first high C in 'chest', in 1837, in Rossini's *William Tell*. Although this achieved a great success with the public, Rossini was less enthusiastic, describing it as 'the squawk of a capon having its throat cut'. Despite Rossini's distaste, the ability to produce ringing high notes became a basic requirement for any aspiring tenor. Although the Italian spinto or dramatic tenor developed his voice to carry considerable weight up to the top, the heaviest tenor voice is the German *Heldentenor* ('heroic tenor'). Wagner encouraged the development of this voice-type not merely to meet his musical demands, but as a voice that would be equal to the expressive and spiritual demands of the newer German music. These expressive qualities he considered at least as important as the attainment of sheer physical power, though that was (and is) vital.

The brilliance demanded of the Italianate tenor voice was also required from the Italian dramatic baritone; in fact the Verdi baritone has to sing almost as high as the *Heldentenor*. The German tradition favoured a lower-lying baritone, or bass-baritone, with more sonority in the middle and lower registers. In general the French school of singing displayed more restraint than the Italian. A typical French voice would be more highly placed than its German counterpart, and would take less weight up to the highest notes, even using falsetto – as was the case with Jean-Blaise Martin, who gave his name to the lighter French baritone known as 'baryton Martin'.

It should be remembered that in the nineteenth and early twentieth centuries most singers sang contemporary music, usually of one type, depending on their nationality or where they worked. Nowadays singers have to master music of all periods and styles: even early music specialists who might once have restricted themselves to Baroque music now sing a more varied repertoire. There is therefore a more general, international (some would say anonymous) style and sound employed in the world's opera houses than one hears on the earliest recordings. However, now as then, the greatest singers are those who are instantly recognizable, with an individual sound and personality, and not ' just another' soprano or tenor.

Voice training today

The principles of bel canto are no less relevant today; and, quite apart from being indispensable to a stylistic interpretation of nineteenth-century music, they form an ideal basis for any young singer. As for deliberately aiming for a heavier tone, or trying to fit one of the categories of voice mentioned above, this is never to be recommended. If a voice has the potential for a dark dramatic sound, this will come naturally with maturity.

Many young singers of today (including many of those who eventually have solo careers) start out singing in choirs and consorts. For those from such a background the principles of bel canto are particularly appropriate. First of all, the 'straight' choral sound is ultimately not suitable for classical solo singing. Any breathiness in the tone or in the attack is also to be discouraged. The tone should be as clean as possible, thus ensuring an economical use of the breath. If the singer can maintain a cleanness of production and resist overloading, or pushing with breath, the tone will then be forward, and vibrant.

On the question of vibrato, it is true to say that a large proportion of opera singers these days sing with more vibrato than did their nineteenth-century counterparts. This has led many of those in the field of early music to react by asking for no vibrato whatsoever. However, any healthily produced vocal sound has a degree of oscillation. If you listen to the earliest recordings, you will hear an often almost imperceptible vibrato, narrower and faster than that produced by many present-day opera singers. Even in the more dramatic nineteenth-century voices the vibrato is more brilliant (often almost flickering) than the slower twentieth-century equivalent. If a young singer can maintain a well supported, forward tone and resist aiming for power for its own sake, then he or she should avoid the development of a wobble or tremolo.

Absolutely necessary for a convincing performance of the nineteenth-century solo repertoire is the cultivation of a perfect legato. Manuel García not only stresses the importance of a legato in which the voice passes smoothly from one note to the next, but also recommends the practise of sostenuto, or slurred tones, in which each note is joined to the next with a portamento. Jenny Lind is documented as having practised passing through every semitone, gradually speeding up the slur so that it becomes imperceptible, leaving perfectly bound tones (Ex. 6.1). Singers from a choral background or used to singing Baroque music may find they need to work quite hard to perfect their legato. Quite apart from the fact that they are accustomed to a more clinical way of singing, the problem is sometimes a matter of taste. However, they must come to terms with this, and learn to let go!

Ex. 6.1. Jenny Lind's vocal exercise for legato-sostenuto.

The same is true of the portamento in which, spanning a larger interval, the voice is carried through an infinite number of pitches. The portamento is usually an anticipation of the note it approaches, as in Ex. 6.2a from Vaccai's *Metodo pratico di canto italiano per camera* of 1832, a work that cannot be too highly recommended from both a historical and a practical point of view. Vaccai also discusses a second type of portamento (Ex. 6.2b), which in effect involves starting the second note from below, though with the proviso that this type should not be overdone. It is worth spending some time mastering the execution of this indispensable feature of nineteenth-century music, so that it doesn't come out as an uncontrolled slide or scoop – thus giving ammunition to those who advocate a more clinical (and mistaken!) approach to nineteenth-century repertoire. Another feature that such a clinical approach would prohibit is the use of the *aspirate* (a lightly-voiced 'h': see Ex. 6.4) as a feature of a legato phrase.

(a)

Vor - rei   spie-gar   l'af - fan - no

Ex. 6.2. N. Vaccai, *Metodo pratico di canto italiano per camera* (1832): (a) the portamento; (b) a second type of portamento.

(b)

o   pla - ci-do il   ma - re lu - sin-ghi la spon-da

Another important feature of the bel canto phrase, along with the portamento, is the *messa di voce*, or crescendo–diminuendo. Throughout the history of singing this has been used as an exercise to help develop the steadiest tone and control of the breath. In any broad legato aria of the bel canto repertoire, the line should be shaped by means of the *messa di voce*, producing an ever-changing range of colours, the range of which is limited only by the singer's musical imagination. This bel canto manner of moulding the vocal line is closely allied to the rubato and rhythmic freedom that is discussed in the next section (see also Exx. 6.3 and 6.4).

Ex. 6.3. M. García, *Traité complet de l'art du chant* (1840–47). Portamento with inflections, from G. Rossini, *Il barbiere di Siviglia* (1816).

Ex. 6.4. G. Donizetti, *L'elisir d'amore* (1832). Extract showing several typical features of nineteenth-century vocal style, including aspiration.

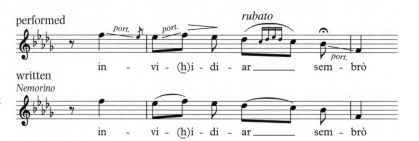

The other crucial aspect of bel canto singing is the mastery of coloratura. Many singers who have taken part in the performance of a Baroque work such as Handel's *Messiah*, either as soloist or in the chorus, will already be aware of the demands of florid music. In Romantic music the coloratura probably needs to be sung with more voice, and often more legato, though the faster passages in Rossini, especially in the tenor roles, require the same sort of articulation in the throat that is demanded by Monteverdi. This does not mean a throaty tone, nor anything other than the most forward 'placing'. It is especially important not to overload with the breath. The idea of performing runs 'from the diaphragm' is not a very useful one, if we are going to achieve real velocity and virtuosity. Again the exercises of Vaccai provide ideal training for various types of coloratura.

Evidence of national styles

For music composed before 1850 we have only written evidence as to how it might have been performed. However, in the case of later music, we can support the written evidence with recordings of singers who were performing during the second half of the century. Adelina Patti, for example, who can be heard on recordings made around 1905, made her adult début (at the age of sixteen!) in 1859. By studying the written sources, the most comprehensive of which is García's *Traité*, in the light of these recordings, we can build up a fairly clear idea of nineteenth-century performing style. Up to the middle of the nineteenth century, the style of performance of the Italian singing tradition applied equally to French opera. As the century progressed different national styles became more established. In the case of the German and French repertoires, the text was much more strictly adhered to. Within the Italian tradition, the history of performance can be seen as a progression from the highly florid early Romantic style to the very strictly notated operas of Puccini. In a short chapter it is not possible to document the rapid changes that took place between 1830 and 1900, though what follows should give a general idea of some of the characteristics of the Romantic singing style.

The Italian tradition

If we listen to some of the earliest recordings, perhaps following the score, probably the first thing we notice (after we have got used to the sound quality) is the rhythmic freedom. In fact we notice many of the things that nowadays are frowned upon, such as speeding up in the more excited passages and slowing down at cadences. What may be written as a passage of even quavers may come out as anything but this. Dotted rhythms may be double-dotted (the usual practice) or, in a more expressive aria, sung as triplets. In Italian arias there may be a certain amount of decoration, as in Patti's 1906 recording of 'Ah! non credea' from Bellini's *La sonnambula* (Ex. 6.5). As Patti studied with musicians who had been involved in the first performances of some of Bellini's operas, we can take her style of perform- ance as historically authentic – though she is actually quite restrained in comparison with earlier generations, as can be seen from the elaborations by Maria Malibran (Ex. 6.6). However, Patti's version offers a good starting point for a young singer of today who wishes to investigate authentic nineteenth-century performance practice. And it won't shock critics (or examiners!) too much!

Ex. 6.5. V. Bellini, *La sonnambula* (1831), 'Ah! non credea', as recorded by Adelina Patti.

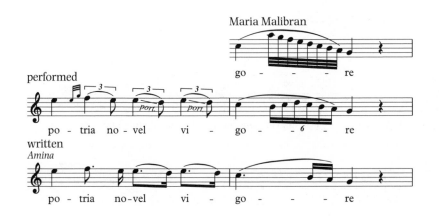

Ex. 6.6. M. García, *Traité complet de l'art du chant*. Extract showing elaboration by Maria Malibran (transposed), from V. Bellini, *La sonnambula*, 'Ah! non credea'.

Tempo rubato

If we look further back in the century, we see an even greater degree of freedom, indeed an often quite considerable deviation from the written score. This freedom frequently takes the form of 'tempo rubato', where the accompaniment remains more or less in time while the melody is treated more freely, with certain notes being prolonged and others shortened. As can be seen in the following examples (Ex. 6.7), the stress of the words must be maintained.

(a)

(b)

(c)

Ex. 6.7. M. García, *Traité complet de l'art du chant*. Extracts showing use of tempo rubato, from:
(a) G. Donizetti, *Anna Bolena* (1830);
(b) G. Rossini, *La gazza ladra* (1817);
(c) N. A. Zingarelli, *Giulietta e Romeo* (1796);
(d) G. Rossini, *La donna del lago* (1819).

(d)

The appoggiatura

García wrote that in Italian singing the appoggiatura can scarcely be considered an ornament, as it is a means of preserving the word stress, and as such is obligatory. Italian, though a more legato language than English, has strong accents, usually on the penultimate syllable of a phrase: this is reflected in the use of the appoggiatura. Not only in recitatives but frequently also in arias, if the composer ends a phrase by writing two notes of the same pitch, the first of which is a strong syllable and the second weak, then an appoggiatura is called for (Exx. 6.8a and b). The practice of adding appoggiaturas continued well into the last quarter of the century, though Verdi, for example, began to write out what might previously have been singers' interpolations, as in Ex. 6.9.

Exx. 6.8a and b. G. Donizetti, *L'elisir d'amore*. Appoggiaturas in recitative.

Ex. 6.9. G. Verdi, *La traviata* (1853). Written-out appoggiaturas reflecting word stress.

The fermata

At important cadences, such as at the end of a section where the composer writes a pause, the singer was expected to execute a cadenza. In the nineteenth century, this point in the aria was an opportunity for the singer to show off not only inventiveness but also virtuosity, as shown in Exx. 6.10 and 6.11.

Ex. 6.10. M. García, *Traité complet de l'art du chant*. A fermata, described by García as a 'good example', from D.-F.-E. Auber, *Le serment* (1832).

Ex. 6.11. G. Nava (1802–75), *Metodo pratico di canto*. Fermatas: these are somewhat restrained compared to Ex. 6.10.

General alterations

It is not only at cadences that the singer could indulge in some vocal display. In an aria, especially one in a virtuoso style, if an idea is repeated it would be normal to vary the vocal line. Of course this should always be according to the expression. Opposite (Ex. 6.12) are some examples from García including, you may be surprised to see, a recitative (Ex. 6.12d). You may find it useful to follow García's advice and practise inventing such alterations, as well as cadenzas.

In plainer, simpler melodies there should be a less extravagant interpretation. The next example from García (Ex. 6.13) shows a possible interpre-

Ex. 6.12. M. García, *Traité complet de l'art du chant*. Extracts showing possible versions of passages from Rossini operas: (a) *La donna del lago*; (b) and (c) *Tancredi* (1813); (d) *Otello* (1816).

Ex. 6.13. M. García, *Traité complet de l'art du chant*. Possible interpretation of a cantabile melody, from D. Cimarosa, *Il matrimonio segreto* (1792), tenor aria.

tation of a simple cantabile melody. Though the original comes from an earlier period, the style of performance is very much of the mid-nineteenth century. The example could serve as a guide to singers who wish to investigate this style of performance. Notice that the decorations tend to take place on strong syllables. Note also the appoggiaturas at the ends of phrases.

The German tradition

If we compare the music of the German tradition with the Italian, it is clear that there is less opportunity for actually varying the vocal line. The Italian arias most suitable for elaboration usually have a fairly straightforward accompaniment, with the main burden of the drama and expression being borne by the vocal line (and thus by the singer). By the time we get to Wagner, we see a much more important role for the orchestra, the voice often seeming to be merely another instrument. Similarly in the lieder repertoire the piano is often at least as important as the vocal line. This greatly limits the freedom of the singer, at least as regards alterations: even appoggiaturas are often written out. However, this does not mean that performers adopted the rhythmically strict style prevalent today. Nineteenth-century performances of the lieder repertoire were rhythmically much freer than today's.

The legato that formed the basis of bel canto should also form the basis for the singing of the German song repertoire. The original interpreters of many of the German songs of the repertoire of today's singer would have used a good deal of portamento, as well as inflecting and colouring the vocal line by the use of *messa di voce*. In comparison to the modern school of lieder singing exemplified by Dietrich Fischer-Dieskau and Elisabeth Schwarzkopf, the expression would be conveyed more through the musical

Ex. 6.14. (overleaf) J. Brahms, *Feldeinsamkeit* ('In Summer Fields') Op. 86 No. 2, 1882. Square brackets show interpretation by Gustav Walter, who transposed the song from F to A major.

phrase and vocal inflections of a bel canto line, rather than characterizing every verbal effect, often to the detriment of the vocal line. Again, as in the case of the Italian tradition, increases of emotion often brought about an increase of tempo, and a relaxation of emotion a corresponding rallentando. At the final cadence of a song there was often what we would now consider a considerable rallentando; in fact just the sort of slowing down, or even a pause on the penultimate note, that we are now taught not to do!

In considering the style of lieder performance, we are fortunate in having recorded evidence. The Bohemian singer Gustav Walter was born in 1834, and his singing was known to Brahms, who by all accounts approved of it. In 1904 he recorded a number of songs including Brahms's *Feldeinsamkeit*. Ex. 6.14 (pp. 84–5) shows this song, annotated to show Walter's interpretation. Listening to this recording, one is struck by two main characteristics. First, there is copious use of portamento, with the second note anticipated. However, in the second verse, the line *mir ist, als ob ich längst gestorben bin* ('it is as if I had long since died') is sung more plainly, without portamento, so as to express the sentiment. This is more in keeping with modern taste, though you may find the slight sobbing a little too much! The other feature of the interpretation which immediately strikes a modern listener is the flexibility of tempo. Apart from the customary ritardandos, the singer obviously gains sheer vocal pleasure in his expansive singing of the broad, arched phrases. In fact, once you are accustomed to the licence which Walter takes, it is hard to go back to singing the song *a tempo*. Walter's interpretation could serve as a model for those wishing to pursue a freer manner of singing the lyrical songs of Brahms, Schumann and Wolf. Of course, in the more declamatory and narrative songs a simpler musical approach is more appropriate: in these the singer needs to use all his or her imagination to characterize the text and bring it to life as would an actor.

The flexibility of tempo that we hear in Walter's singing of Brahms corresponds to descriptions of Wagner's performances of his own and other composers' music. He would vary the tempo according to the dramatic and emotional content. Cantabile passages would be taken very broadly, while more lively passages would be taken at a quicker tempo. In fact Walter's approach in Brahms, both musically and in his manner of singing, is entirely consistent with the recorded evidence of those singers who worked with Wagner. The oldest Wagnerian tenor who made recordings is Hermann Winkelmann (born in 1849). He uses portamento in rather the same way as Walter, and there is something similar in his soulful delivery and in the way he ends certain phrases with the same sort of sob. The fact that this 'sobbing' can be heard in a number of singers of his generation suggests that it was an accepted part of their style of singing, and not merely an untidy or uncontrolled vocal release.

Listening to Winkelmann and others who worked at Bayreuth, such as Lilli Lehmann and Marianne Brandt, one becomes aware that they sang with less vibrato than many modern singers of this repertoire. Also, the earliest Heldentenors on record sing with less pressure than many of those of the last few decades, placing their voices higher instead of pushing an almost baritonal quality as high as possible. In fact, although Wagner explicitly wished to create German art, with singing that produced 'nobler passions' and a 'spiritual significance' that went beyond the 'mere sensuous pleasure' of Italian vocalism, his idea of what constitutes good singing is quite consistent with bel canto.

Of course, the German language behaves quite differently from Italian. Many syllables end in consonants, and there are many consonant clusters that do not occur in Italian. German, a 'stress-timed' language like English (with syllables of varying lengths), tends to fall into strong beats, which can contain (usually) two or three syllables. The use of the glottal stop, which does not occur in Italian, helps to reinforce the 'beats' of the language. Although in Wagner the declamation of the text is of the utmost importance, in his setting of the text he has already attempted to preserve as much as possible the 'spoken accent' of the words in the musical setting. Therefore it is up to the singer, instead of emphasizing further the aspects of the language mentioned above, merely(!) to sing clearly and precisely what is written. And, rather than weighting the consonants at the expense of the vowels, as happens all too often in Wagner performances, he or she must use the vowel tone to communicate the emotional power of the word or idea being expressed. The consonants in German are heavier than in Italian or French, and many of the voiced consonants can be used to preserve the legato.

The French tradition

As with the German tradition, the development of opera in nineteenth-century France shows a gradual move away from the Italian style. The Italian influence was still strong up to the 1830s, not surprisingly given that Rossini moved to Paris in 1824, as director of the Théâtre-Italien, bringing with him a number of Italian singers. However his French operas, *Le Comte Ory* and *William Tell*, reveal a much plainer style of vocal writing, still lyrical in the Italian manner, but combined with the more declamatory style that has been such an important characteristic of French opera from Lully onwards. This plainer vocal style, together with a sense of spectacle – also an important thread in the history of French opera – was a crucial element in the development of the 'grand operas' of Meyerbeer, which sought to express human passions against the backdrop of a historical drama.

The operas of Meyerbeer, despite their plainer style, still contain cadenzas, though these are written out, and tend to be less elaborate than corresponding examples in Italian bel canto. While it is likely that singers in the earlier decades of the nineteenth century would still have sung with considerable freedom, and even some elaboration of what the composer wrote, in the works of Gounod, Bizet and Massenet a much stricter adherence to the score is called for. It should be remembered, however, that what a nineteenth-century singer considered strict, or *a tempo*, was less *a tempo* than what we are used to nowadays! For example, the soprano Emma Eames, who studied the part of Juliette in Gounod's *Romeo et Juliette* with the composer, stated in a radio talk that Gounod had insisted on her singing in strict time without any uncalled-for ritardandos. However, her recording of the aria is extremely free, with a lot of ritardandos! Whether this is what the composer really wanted, or whether over time Eames became less vigilant in these matters, it is impossible to say. Perhaps Gounod's conception was somewhere in between Eames's very liberal realization and a late twentieth-century idea of strictness. There is no doubt, however, that Gounod required a somewhat more precise realization than was normal in early nineteenth-century Italian opera. And it is true that late nineteenth- and early twentieth-century performances of French repertoire often sound surprisingly modern, apart from employing a cleaner and less forced vocal production than is all too common today.

Crucial to the idiomatic performance of French vocal music, then as now, is an awareness of the importance of the text. Gounod's vocal lines respect closely the prosody of the libretto. The text is equally important in the music of Massenet, though the latter achieved a more Italianate lyricism by allowing the vocal line more freedom. (The relatively unstressed French language allows this free setting.) However, open a score of Massenet's *Werther*, and you will see that virtually every note of the vocal line is set to a new syllable (see Ex. 6.15): nowhere will you find the melismas of the Italian bel canto operas. This is as true in fast, dramatic sections as in slower, more cantabile passages.

Ex. 6.15.
J. Massenet, *Werther* (1892). Note Massenet's detailed marking of the vocal line.

In performance, this could bring about a choppy way of singing. It is therefore vital to respect the characteristics of the French language. As in Italian and Spanish, but not in English and German, almost every syllable in French ends in a vowel sound, while the consonants must never be sung at all heavily. The implication of this is that every vowel must be sung for as long as possible to fill the duration of each note. This applies to smaller note values as well as to longer notes. It is also important not to stress the words as one might when singing in Italian. In French all the syllables are almost equally accented, and the accent on the final syllable of a word or word group is realized more by duration than by a heavy stress as in English. Any pointing of words has to be achieved with subtlety and without unnecessary heavy accents. By respecting the characteristics of the language in this way, even at its most lyrical French opera will always be more restrained than its Italian counterpart. Thus Italian music has been described as more passionate and elastic, French as more aristocratic.

Mélodies

All the comments above concerning the style of French music, especially as regards the relationship of the text and vocal line, are applicable to the performance of the French song repertoire. With piano accompaniment instead of orchestra and therefore with the vocal line more exposed, the precise realization of the text becomes even more important. This does not mean speaking on pitch, or parlando-type delivery. Every syllable should be sung for its full length, and every nuance marked by the composer observed within the context of the basic legato. Heavy downbeats should be avoided, unless specifically asked for. None of this implies any sort of mechanical performance. Once the singer has achieved as near perfect a legato as possible, in which the horizontal aspect of the music is emphasized rather than the vertical, he or she can allow subtle rhythmical nuances. For instance, in Ex. 6.16, if the shorter notes are stretched to their limit so that occasionally the following consonant is almost late, thus avoiding a strong vertical accent with the accompaniment, this can help depict the floating ships and the rocking of the cradles.

Ex. 6.16. G. Fauré, *Les berceaux* Op. 23 No. 1, 1879, bb. 3–7.

Gounod once made a distinction between 'articulation', which 'has for its object to reproduce faithfully the exterior form of the word', and 'pronunciation', which 'imparts to the word the thought, the sentiment, the passion, in which it is enveloped'. The singer should use the vowels to express the meaning and sentiment of the word. And especially in the songs of Debussy, he or she must be able to produce the most sensuous colours, often conveying the deepest emotions while observing all the musical details (see Ex. 6.17). While in the vocal music of Fauré and

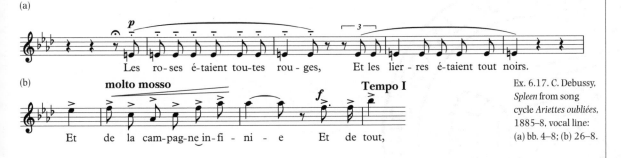

Ex. 6.17. C. Debussy, *Spleen* from song cycle *Ariettes oubliées*, 1885–8, vocal line: (a) bb. 4–8; (b) 26–8.

Debussy the emotion may be less obvious than in Wagner and Verdi, if the singer can achieve the right balance of passion and reason the result should be equally affecting.

Conclusion

It is hardly necessary to mention that one of the most important responsibilities of the singer in the Romantic opera and song repertoire, as in any other, is the communication of the dramatic and emotional implications of the music and text. But even here we may note some differences between the performances of a nineteenth-century singer and that of his or her modern counterpart. Along with the rhythmic freedom of the earlier performances, we find a freedom of expression which often makes many modern performances seem rather inhibited. This is particularly true in music of the Italian tradition. It is very likely that if we travelled back in time we would find vocal performances rather uncontrolled and over-emotional; indeed modern singers would find it somewhat excessive, if not downright embarrassing, to include sobs (considered quite a valid effect by García) in their performances. It is clear that modern singers who are serious about trying to recreate something of the real nineteenth-century style will have to evaluate their tastes as well as their musical and artistic habits. However, even a degree of the freedom allowed to their earlier counterparts will almost certainly help their general vocal ability, as well as stimulate their imagination.

As yet, none of the well-known early music conductors has attempted to realize the implications of the sources which form the basis for this chapter. Perhaps the more enterprising of the next generation of singers will help develop an authentic nineteenth-century style of performance which will cast new light on a familiar repertoire, as has happened in the music of earlier centuries.

Robert Pascall

Sources
and Editions

Text and context

E. M. Forster began his famous novel *Howards End* with the motto 'Only connect...'; and it is important for us as performers to understand, in as fine-grained a way as possible, the role of the written text of a composition within the activity of music-making. This might seem initially like nit-picking, or trying to make difficulties where, in common sense, none exist: but let me attempt to persuade you otherwise. If we stop to think what a piece of music actually is, then something of the intricacy of the connections involved becomes apparent. Is the piece what the composer conceived, what he or she wrote down, what was printed, how it was performed at the time of its composition, how people then heard it, what is printed today, how it is performed and how heard today?

The obvious answer of course is that it is all of these things: we call by a single title something which has indeed all these manifestations, hoping that the title represents a real identity. In some sense our hope must be justified, but the disparities of those manifestations are clearly fairly extreme. Composers work with aural imagination: when creating, they hear their emerging pieces perhaps mainly in their heads, like Brahms, or perhaps by working at an instrument, as Chopin did on the piano. The writing down is then a fixing of the piece in a medium which only rather crudely represents sounds, and the composer's 'interpretation' – how precisely he heard the work in his head or on his own piano – begins to make way for other interpretations by other interpreters.

It is clear that at least some of Brahms's wrestling with notation (his scores are often heavily corrected) resulted not from lack of certainty about his imagination, but from lack of certainty about the best way of using notation to capture what he imagined, the best way of 'getting the message across'. And, as we shall see, for many of Chopin's works we have a radically quite different situation: he left for us several equally valid notations of the same piece.

Every performance is different, and of course a composer gives his work for interpretation by others, happily letting go of the specificity of the sounds he imagined. But let us stay with the idea of those sounds for a moment: they were, naturally, imagined by the composer in terms of the instrumental or vocal tone, playing or singing techniques and interpretative styles of his time. Even if the composer had posterity in mind, as composers often did in that historically aware age – Brahms for instance aimed to compose what he called 'durable' music – these sonic values must be explicitly or implicitly (depending on your view) incorporated in the notation the composer chose. Matters of crucial importance to performers would have been understood as part of that text by him and his contemporaries: improvised ornamentation and expressive nuancing of tempo and dynamics are two areas which spring immediately to mind. And if one is tempted to think that neither of these really applies to nineteenth-century music, one is simply wrong. In spite of nineteenth-century notation carrying more information than any previous notation, improvised embellishment was characteristically added by singers of Italian opera, portamento and vibrato (as ornament) by string players, spread chords and melody desynchronized from its accompaniment by pianists. Rubato and expressive freedom are points often noted by contemporary commentators on the playing of Chopin and Brahms; and Liszt and Wagner thought of tempo modification as an essential expressive device, associating it particularly with changes of theme and harmony.

All this leads us to the first maxim for performers approaching a text: *notation is of its time and place and can only be properly understood in terms of the performance practices of that time and place.* But let us stop here too: we cannot fully recapture those performance practices, and, even if we could, we are interpreters living in our own time, with our own ideals and audiences. So that leads us swiftly to the second maxim: *our historical knowledge is always partial and serves only ever as context for our own interpretations; in this way such knowledge becomes freeing rather than binding for our interpretative ideas and skills.* But less forbiddingly: what we need today is a general picture of what the notation meant in interpretative terms; this will give us the background for creating our own interpretation, and perhaps a few more interpretative ideas which we are free to use or not.

Since this book is about performance practice, the ways *listeners* perceived and constructed meaning in the nineteenth century will have to be left mostly 'on hold'. This forms a special area of investigation known as 'reception history'. But there were two pervasive strands in the Romantic period which are worth taking on board. The first is what is now known as 'poetizing criticism', and it refers to the way in which writers and listeners then made pictures of musical meaning: Clara Schumann, for instance, described Brahms's Third Symphony as speaking of 'the secret magic of the life of the forest'. This kind of response to music stemmed primarily from the early Romantic critic, novelist and composer E. T. A. Hoffmann, and so prevalent did it become that Liszt in mid-century defined a programme attached to a piece of music in terms of something which essentially sought to *limit* the range of interpretative pictures that could be made. The second strand is the way in which composers and critics related to particular musical genres: arguments would arise as to whether a work was a symphony or a suite – as happened, for instance, with Goldmark's symphony *Ländliche Hochzeit* ('Rustic Wedding') – or whether a concerto was 'symphonic' (it depended on one's view whether this was a plus or a minus), or whether a particular symphony was in essence amplified chamber music. The important point is not the rights and wrongs of the arguments, rather just how conscious the age was of generic issues and of the different types of musical discourse appropriate to the different genres.

Does such knowledge affect us today? Well, it can do, but it needn't. We are free as listeners (and performers are listeners too) to construct musical meaning as we wish, and the play of knowledge, intuition and feeling remains for each of us quite properly a deeply personal matter. Thus we can very well apply our second maxim to listening as well.

Documents: their production and significance

As a piece was worked out and worked on by its composer, various types of written document were generated, emended and polished. Each composer had different working habits, and we have already noted a particular difference between Chopin and Brahms in this regard. Furthermore, composers often treated different pieces differently: the creation of a symphony might start with a sketched theme for instance, that of a song with a rhythmic laying out of words – so we will have to be rather general and schematic in our thinking here.

In the early stages of working out, we might expect working notes and ideas (which may be in project books or letters to friends and relations), sketches (usually testing out important details such as openings, themes or counterpoints) and drafts (more extended than sketches, testing how details belong together in continuity). If the piece is for complicated forces, for instance a large chamber group or orchestra, we might also find a type of draft called a 'particell': that is, a whole movement or work in short score, without the details of instrumentation or textures fully worked out. The documents so far are, from the composer's point of view, means to an end, and different composers had different attitudes to preserving such records of their creative processes. No great composer was more assiduous in keeping his sketches and drafts than Beethoven; Brahms, on the other hand, purposely destroyed his, though a few do survive, for instance on the back of correction slips pasted down in other scores.

Then comes the important stage of the 'first full writing down'; the inverted commas are there because, for editors, this is a technical term for a most significant document. The criterion here is that of completeness. If the composition now exists in what is recognizably its full form, irrespective of whether this is also its final form (often *not* the case!), then we have a key source for the work in its freshest state, and one to which editors have to pay considerable attention, provided, of course, that it survives.

The 'first full writing down' forms what scholars loosely call the autograph of a piece, and it can be more or less messy depending on the composer's handwriting and the amount of correction (in general, Mendelssohn and Chopin were relatively neat, Brahms somewhat messy, Debussy very neat). Autographs of great composers are now treasured and very valuable objects, fetching astronomic prices on the rare occasions they come up at auction. Although several enlightened collectors in the nineteenth century realized their significance and interest, wider acceptance of their importance is a relatively recent phenomenon. Hence it is that a significant number of autographs no longer exist: many of Fauré's song autographs, for instance, are said to have been used as jampot covers by his publisher's wife.

Having written a piece down, the composer then wants it performed, often to test whether it works in practice as he thought it would. If the piece is for more than one or two performers, then a copy or copies of some kind become necessary. Orchestral and chamber music players, choral and ensemble singers need parts, while a solo singer might look over the pianist's shoulder or have her or his own copy. Furthermore, a composer might want his score copied, perhaps because his autograph was already messy and hard to read, or to protect the autograph from overuse or loss; or, in the case of smaller pieces such as songs and piano pieces, to present his latest work to friends. In the days before the photocopier, these copies would be done by hand, perhaps by the composer, often by a professional copyist. (There are a few exceptions to this rule: for instance Brahms had string parts engraved at his own expense for his later orchestral works, at a time when he was relatively wealthy; and choir members sometimes copied their own parts, passing an original from person to person.)

Each of these extra sources after the autograph can bring with it its own problems. What if a composer, copying out a work, makes an inadvertent alteration or an unnoticed slip? What if the parts are improved during rehearsal but not the score? What if the copyist mistakes crucial signs and these go through uncorrected to the engraver? With copies, the criteria for assessing them are: authorization (to what degree did the composer control production?), purpose (were they used by the composer for test performances?; hence do they perhaps carry and transmit his own improvements, whether or not in his own hand?; did they go on to have a further role in the publication of the work?) and quality (how accurate is the text?).

Before the time of Haydn and Mozart, publication was by no means a common aim, even for great composers. J. S. Bach, for instance, published very, very little of his enormous output, and his Op. 1 did not appear until he was forty-six. In the nineteenth century, however, a burgeoning market, together with advances in printing techniques, came to mean that even rather minor composers could expect publication, and major ones could make a reasonable living from it. Publication characteristically happened with the involvement of the composers concerned: the composer would prepare and provide the source for the engraver to use, read proofs and pass the result for publication. This was not, however, always the case: for example, the first edition of Musorgsky's *Pictures at an Exhibition* was produced, just after the composer's death, by his friend and colleague Rimsky-Korsakov, who made his own 'improvements' – doubtless with the best intentions but obviously not with the consent of the composer.

The source provided for the engraver might be the composer's own autograph manuscript or a manuscript copy, such as discussed above. Either way, the engraver had to interpret the writing correctly and then to regulate the text in terms of the printing rules of the time; for instance crescendo and decrescendo hairpins normally started and ended on noteheads (as indeed they still do today). One can just imagine how often engravers got this kind of regulation wrong; they confused certain signs too (*rf* and *sf* for instance), misidentified the staves to which the performance markings should attach, and left some out altogether. These matters are much more common than errors of pitch or rhythm, though those also slipped in from time to time.

Technically the publication of a work divides into two basic processes:

the origination (how the notational image is actually made) and the printing itself (how this image is reproduced in the many copies required). In the period we are considering here, music was mostly printed using engraved plates. Thus the origination would be in the hands of an engraver, gouging and punching the notation into metal sheets, or plates, one for each page. Since the normal method of printing involved pressing the plate into paper, engraving was usually done from right to left, i.e. in mirror image. Engraving involved highly skilled work with many different tools, and it took several hours for a single page of music to be created in this way. Once the whole work had been engraved, printing could commence by filling the engraved lines and notes with ink, wiping the unengraved parts of the plate free of ink, and pressing the plate very hard into clean paper. While this is nothing like a full account of these processes (later printings could, for instance, be made by transferring the image from plate to a lithographic stone), it is important for today's editors to understand something of what happened, for how a plate was made and corrected (with hammer or liquid metal), and how a plate deteriorated under many pressings into many pieces of clean paper (staccato dots and other small signs started to disappear) have a bearing on today's decisions about which textual readings should be preferred.

Fig. 7.1. Punching note-heads into a metal plate.

The composer would correct an early proof copy: but he was, of course, primarily a composer, most probably already working on another piece; and even for non-composers proof-reading is an irksome, time-consuming business. So we can by no means assume that proof-reading was always scrupulously done. But – and here is a real difficulty for editors of nineteenth-century music today – some composers used the proofs to polish their compositions that little bit further. So the manuscript which had been sent for publication, if it survives today, cannot and must not be assumed to contain the composer's final wished-for form of the text. As Brahms wrote to his own publisher about his *Variations on a Theme by J. Haydn* Op. 56a: 'it is not the manuscript that is definitive but rather the engraved score, which I myself have corrected'. Thus today's editor must start from the assumption that the first publication of a piece may well contain both mistakes and improvements.

Surviving proof copies from our period are very rare indeed, for the obvious reason that they were considered as part of a process and not end-products in themselves; once they had served their purpose, they became mere clutter. So the question arises as to why any at all have come down to us. Were they duplicate copies not returned to the publisher? In which case do they necessarily contain exactly those markings the composer wanted taken into the print? First editions do, on the whole, survive, and an important force for their survival was the deposit system used to back up copy-right (The British Library, for instance, forms an excellent resource for editors). The criteria for assessment of proof-copies and first editions are: degree of authorization (just how far was the composer actively involved in controlling the quality of what was done, or did he delegate matters? – this varies from composer to composer and from work to work), and care of production (just how good were the engravers and the control procedures?).

But matters don't stop here. Many composers in our period could not leave their music alone – quite understandably of course: if you, as a composer, decide that your piece sounds better with a different note, or melody, or chord here or there, what more natural than that you should make alterations in your own printed copy of the work? Chopin sets editors a very particular problem in this regard, since he altered compositions in the course of teaching his favourite students – though some students got different alterations from others. Brahms also sets us some problems, since he both altered his own copies (sometimes also those of his friends) and wrote to his publishers to revise the work: but the letters and the marks do not always correlate properly. We shall return to these matters later in two brief case-studies, but let us note here that the criteria for judging post-publication alterations are: validation (do they represent the composer's intentions?) and generality of application (are they meant to alter the text given to the world, or are they for a particular performing occasion, with perhaps particular difficulties of acoustic or playing skills?).

Emendations to an edition could be made without a publisher announcing the fact, so later printings, particularly during the lifetime of a composer, can have real importance. Here again we have to find out if we can, or judge if we can't, just how much the composer has been involved. If a composer makes radical revisions, then a new version of a piece may result, requiring re-engraving, at least in part. This causes no problems for today's editors – they merely publish both versions – but performers have of course to choose which version they are going to perform.

What editors do

After everything that has been said here about documents, it will be abundantly clear that today's editor is in the first instance a historian. He or she must reconstruct, in as fine detail as the surviving sources allow, the sequential stages of the emergence, development and finalization of a written text. Such work involves the assembly of sources, their description, relation and evaluation.

For the assembly of sources, thematic catalogues for individual composers and library catalogues are indispensable: but some manuscripts remain in private hands; others are presumed lost but might be findable by good detective work. One then has to go and see the manuscripts. There are technical rules for their description, involving accounts of their paper types, how the sheets of paper were put together, what writing implements have been used, what information is given apart from the music itself (title, date, instructions to copyist and/or engraver, pagination), who the writer was, what the characteristics of the musical handwriting are, whether corrections are present and of what quality these are (to notes, dynamics, phrasing, etc.). All this information can tell you about when, how and by whom the manuscript was created and for what purposes it was used. And this is essential for building up a picture of the relation of the manuscript to other sources, and hence its role in the history of the work. For printed sources the technical rules are different, and are aimed at defining the appearance and quality of the first edition and those of any relevant subsequent issues and editions: the information on the title page is crucial, including titling, price, publisher's name and address and those of distribution agents, copyright claim, plate number; then comes the caption title, layout and printing method of the music itself.

The relation of sources is worked out from their dates, from information in letters (including those between third parties), diaries and other private papers, and also from detailed work on the sources themselves: for instance, engravers marked where they had got to at the ends of their plates with dashes and/or numbers in the manuscript from which they were engraving, and we can almost always say with certainty whether or not a particular manuscript has been used by an engraver. The important aspects of the relation of sources are their chronology, derivations and correlations, or, in less technical language, what is their ordering in time, which was copied from which, and which was checked against which? Editors make a time-flow chart, known as a stemma, showing these relations with a variety of lines, arrows and other signs. But it is only in the really luxurious scholarly editions that we are allowed to publish such things. If you find one in the edition you are using, you have a serious piece of editorial scholarship in front of you.

The evaluation of a source is really to do with deciding its importance and reliability in the definition and emergence of the musical text. The questions one needs to ask have been alluded to in passing in the previous section: how complete is the text, how much did the composer have to do with the generation and control of the source, what was its essential purpose, how much care has gone into its production, how consistent a record is it of the composer's notational intentions and at what particular stage in the process of composition and publication?

Then the editor becomes a text-critic (while also remaining a historian). What this means is that the editor: i) deciphers the sources, logging the emendations contained within each source – nothing should be left unexplained, and all glued-over patches should be lifted; ii) compares the sources against one another (most easily done in chronological order), note for note, performance-sign for performance-sign, and logs the differences.

The variant readings within and across sources are presented in variant tables – which should be made as user-friendly as possible, for they are inherently forbidding in appearance. In my view, in presenting one's work to the public, it is better to list together all the variants for a particular place in the music, rather than dealing first with one source, then with the next, and so on. The 'together' method is not only more interesting for the reader, but it helps the editor too, for his next task is to decide which particular variant reflects the composer's intentions most closely.

He is still essentially acting as a historian, tracing how and why variants came into being and sorting out mistakes from compositional improvements; but he is now also making decisions on what should be printed in the forthcoming edition. These decisions may be relatively easy: if a later variant in a source controlled by the composer makes musical sense, it is more likely to be an improvement rather than a mistake, and, vice versa, something making less musical sense is likely to be a mistake – but there remain cases where two variants make equal musical sense, and then one has to work from the known habits of the composer and engravers.

The next task is to identify the main source for the new edition, and for most nineteenth-century works this will be one of the following: the composer's autograph, an authorized copy, the first edition, the composer's corrected copy of the first edition, or an authorized and emended later edition made during his lifetime. The main source should be the one having the fewest and/or least serious mistakes in it, in other words the most reliable source for the composer's notational intentions. Then, of course, one corrects the mistakes and – absolutely essential – tells the reader in the critical report exactly what one has done.

Perhaps the most common fault of today's editors of nineteenth- and early twentieth-century music is to 'correct' the printed first edition readings according to the autograph, *without* first assessing the composer's involvement in the publication process and considering the possibility that he made compositional changes at proof. Editors can be attracted into this type of error by the current popularity of published facsimiles of composers' autographs. Another relatively common fault, though thankfully becoming less so, is to mix sources according to personal taste ('I'll take this bar from this edition, this bar from that, another bar from the autograph'). The basis for this kind of mixing is purely whimsical, and it is now quite properly considered a real error, for it is not founded on evaluation of sources and it cannot produce a version of the piece ever considered valid by the composer.

We may well come to think that current editorial methods for nineteenth-century music do not pay enough attention to performance practice issues. The essential editorial task of course remains centred on notation, and it is the notational intentions of the composer which lie at the heart of editors' concerns. But what the notation meant to the composer and his contemporaries is a most significant matter, and I hope for the day when editors of nineteenth-century music will offer the equivalent of what their counterparts of earlier music do already, in terms of description of instruments, accounts of playing styles, ornaments, comments on contemporary performances, etc.

Two case-studies

In common with a number of composers in the first half of the nineteenth century, Chopin liked to publish his music simultaneously in different countries, using different publishers: this was the way then of ensuring maximum copyright protection. He published in France, Germany and England, and he would therefore need three copies of each work to generate the publications. Chopin might use a copyist, or he might prepare for publication with his French publisher (usually Schlesinger), then, on receiving proofs or advance copies, send these out – presumably corrected – to his German publishers (Breitkopf & Härtel, or Kistner) and to his publisher in England (Wessel). We will have to wait for detailed research on each individual publication to understand how quite significant variant readings came about, including differences of phrasing, slurs, ties, staccato dots, accents, dynamics, pedalling and notes. Then, after publication, Chopin annotated his own and his pupils' copies with extra ornamentation, fingering and pedalling, and sometimes even quite extensive changes of notes. Ex. 7.1, an illustration of this, is from a copy of Nocturne Op. 15 No. 1 which belonged to Jane Stirling, one of Chopin's most important pupils. We can see how this copy has notes altered and fingering added in Chopin's own hand. But it is clear that he was inconsistent in these additions between pupils, so two particularly interesting questions arise: how far are these additions tailor-made for individual circumstance and therefore lacking durable significance? And how far do the discrepancies represent aspects of Chopin's own interpretative freedom, especially in the matter of the actual notes? We know from reports both how he used to add improvised ornamentation in his own performances and how he liked each performance to be discernibly individual and distinct. The way forward for editors is surely to recognize the plurality of texts he left us for a particular piece, but to choose a single main source as the basis for an intended edition, correcting mistakes and listing variants: the mixing of sources is, even in this extreme case, still not a serious option!

Brahms, working after stricter copyright laws had been introduced in mid-century, published with just one publisher at a time for each piece.

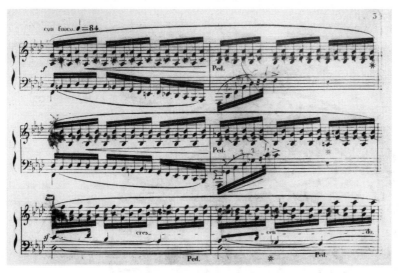

Ex. 7.1. F. Chopin, Nocturne Op. 15 No. 1, 1830–32, bb. 25–30, from Jane Stirling's copy, with annotations by the composer.

Early on in his career he used Breitkopf & Härtel, Senff, Simrock, Rieter-Biedermann and others, but from mid-career Simrock became his main publisher, with a few later works published by Peters. In 1888 Simrock bought up the rights of those pieces earlier published by Breitkopf & Härtel, and invited Brahms to revise these works if he wanted (his most radical revision was of the Piano Trio Op. 8). Normally, Brahms saw his works through the press, correcting proofs and validating the first edition. He then corrected and emended texts in his personal copies of the prints but, after his death, so on occasion did other users.

The marks in his personal copies therefore present something of a difficulty for editors. The first issue to decide is whether a particular mark is in Brahms's hand. For notes, and for cases where Brahms has commented in the margin, this is relatively straightforward, but, especially as far as articulation marks are concerned, we cannot always be certain. Other marks accentuate what is already in the print, Brahms just making the notation more visible for himself on the conductor's podium. Yet others are evidence of an experimental reading, as shown in Ex. 7.2 below, an excerpt from the composer's copy of the song *Sind es Schmerzen*. (In this case we know from

Ex. 7.2. J. Brahms, *Sind es Schmerzen* Op. 33 No. 3, 1861, bb. 65–77, from the composer's copy, with his annotations.

a letter to the publisher that he ultimately preferred the printed reading, though most modern editions wrongly take in the altered version.) Then there are corrections of printing errors, and marks which show compositional improvements. Some of these improvements were carried fully through by writing to the publisher concerned, others not, and for this latter type we have to judge whether they were for a specific occasion or whether Brahms meant them to have general validity. Here Brahms's habits as a letter-writer come into the equation, and there is hard evidence that he was sometimes very slow in writing about changes he really wanted. For us as editors, therefore, real subtlety of judgement is required in each case. Once again the rules apply: give the variants, and tell readers what you have done; then, if a reader disagrees, remedy is at hand, and he or she can find a justified alternative reading.

Types of edition

When the kind of work described above is recorded in full in an introduction and a critical report, it is usually in the context of a modern Collected Edition, which is often described as a Historical/Critical Edition. The collected edition movement began in the nineteenth century itself, as musicians became much more aware of the music of past ages; the first of the great collected editions was the old Bach Complete Edition, begun in 1851. It was followed by editions of Palestrina, Schütz, Handel, Mozart, Beethoven, Schubert, Chopin, Mendelssohn, Schumann and others. New collected editions of many major composers from the period we are considering are currently in progress: Berlioz, Chopin, Schumann, Liszt, Verdi, Wagner, Bruckner, Brahms, Dvořák, Grieg, Elgar, Mahler, Debussy. But there are surprising gaps: there are, for instance, no collected editions for Franck, Smetana, Bizet or Fauré, among others. Volumes in today's collected editions tend to be very expensive indeed, and the place to find them therefore is in really good music libraries. However, the note-texts of their nineteenth- and early twentieth-century predecessors are reproduced in some of the excellent Dover reprint series, though one usually has to do without the full critical reports.

Collected editions are often contrasted with practical editions, but this is a glib, not to say misleading, distinction. Editors of collected editions seek to present the best note-text they can arrive at, representing as closely as possible the notational intentions of the composer. Performers should really be willing to use this as the preferred basis of their study. The work done on collected editions, as we have already seen, is detailed and painstaking, and it is no surprise therefore that they are often used as the source for subsequent editions, perhaps in more practical (more 'music-stand-friendly') format. A kind of lesser sister of the collected edition, whether or not actually derived from a collected edition, is the Urtext edition. As with many important concepts in German, translation is not straightforward, and 'Urtext' implies a mixture of ideas contained in the following English words: a text which is basic, fundamental, primary, stripped of accretions. But we must also realize that the term has now become something of a marketing ploy: a number of Urtext editions of piano music have fingering and/or pedalling added by living performers –

this does not necessarily make them bad editions, of course, but the term Urtext does seem arbitrarily applied.

The quality of an edition really depends on two issues: the quality of the editorial decisions in assessing the sources, and the clarity with which the editor tells you what has been done. The first of these is often very hard indeed for a non-specialist to assess, and one has to take other people's word; the second can be assessed relatively easily by reading the title-page (where, for instance, additional fingering will very probably be attributed) together with the preface or critical report, where an editor should tell you what methods have been followed, and, if the edition is a really good one, list variant readings. As we have seen, for nineteenth-century music, it is most important that the editor does not automatically give the manuscript priority over the first edition.

As performers we want the printed notes we use to be as legible and as well laid out as possible, including conveniently placed page-turns. These considerations are of course entirely different from the issue of quality of textual information which we have been discussing so far. Many performers I know choose a serviceable edition in that visual and practical sense and then consult others, especially those in relevant collected editions, marking up their chosen serviceable edition as necessary. The Dover reprint series is an excellent resource: in the cases of some composers the first editions have been taken, for instance for Wolf, Fauré, Debussy, and in the cases of others collected editions have been reproduced, for instance for Liszt and Brahms. However, Dover does not publish parts for its chamber music volumes. Henle editions, the Wiener Urtext editions and ABRSM editions when done by a named editor are also excellent, and a mark of their quality is the amount of prose material describing the sources, editorial method and decisions.

Envoi

I am sometimes asked why I edit. Among the many reasons are: editing is interesting, challenging, fun; furthermore, it nurtures other forms of musicology – history, criticism, analysis, performance practice research, for instance. But there is really just the one paramount, all-important reason: today's performers should have from working musicologists the most accurate versions achievable of the texts of great music. The editor has the onerous task of establishing in this way the clearest possible lines of communication between the composer on the one hand and you, the interpreter, on the other, enabling the music to live in sound – and hence to be enjoyed – as its creator intended and wished.

Suggestions for Further Reading

The focal point of serious musical study in the English language is *The New Grove Dictionary of Music and Musicians* (London: Macmillan). Good libraries should have the second edition of 2001. In this, the article 'Performing practice' includes a section on performance styles in the nineteenth century, and its bibliography gives details of many of the original sources cited by contributors to this volume. Also useful are the articles on individual instruments, which include descriptions of how the instruments developed, many illustrations, and again detailed bibliographies. In addition to its printed format, *New Grove II* is now available to subscribers on-line: if you can get access to this version through a school, college or library, you can check subject areas such as 'Performing practice' for revisions and updates.

A handy introductory history of the period is Rey M. Longyear's *Nineteenth-Century Romanticism in Music*, 3rd edn (Englewood Cliffs, N. J.: Prentice-Hall, 1988). More detailed are Alfred Einstein's *Music in the Romantic Era* (New York: W. W. Norton & Company; London: Dent, 1947), and two volumes of The New Oxford History of Music, *IX: Romanticism (1830–1890)* and *X: The Modern Age (1890–1960)* (Oxford University Press, 1990; 1974). There is a broad overview of the period in Carl Dahlhaus's *Nineteenth-Century Music*, translated by J. Bradford Robinson (Berkeley: University of California Press, 1989). The most recent scholarship is reflected in *The Cambridge History of Nineteenth-Century Music*, edited by Jim Samson (Cambridge University Press, 2002).

A general study of performing is *Musical Performance: A Guide to Understanding*, edited by John Rink (Cambridge University Press, 2002). Two useful introductions to historically informed interpretation are the New Grove Handbook *Performance Practice: Music after 1600*, edited by Howard Mayer Brown and Stanley Sadie (Basingstoke: Macmillan, 1989), and *The Historical Performance of Music: An Introduction*, edited by Colin Lawson and our contributor Robin Stowell (Cambridge University Press, 1999).

Clive Brown, the author of our chapter on Notation and Interpretation, has written a full-length study of *Classical and Romantic Performing Practice 1750–1900* (Oxford: Clarendon Press, 1999). One important aspect of Romantic performance practice is covered in detail in Richard Hudson's *Stolen Time: The History of Tempo Rubato* (Oxford: Clarendon Press, 1996). There are many general lessons to be learned from *Performing Brahms: Early Evidence of Performance Style*, edited by Michael Musgrave and Bernard D. Sherman (Cambridge University Press, 2002). The recorded evidence of Romantic performing traditions is examined in Robert Philip's *Early Recordings and Musical Style: Changing Tastes in Instrumental Performance, 1900–1950* (Cambridge University Press, 1992).

The Historical Performance of Music: An Introduction, mentioned above, is the introductory volume in a series of more specialist Cambridge Handbooks, all subtitled 'A Practical Guide'. Volumes which have appeared so far (don't be put off by the word 'Early', which extends as far as the nineteenth century) are *Early Keyboard Instruments* by David Rowland (2001), *The Early Violin and Viola* by Robin Stowell (2001), *The Early Clarinet* by Colin Lawson (2000), and *The Early Horn* by John Humphries (2000).

Cambridge University Press has also published a series of companions to different instruments (including the voice), more general in scope but still written largely from a historical perspective. The series includes: *The Cambridge Companion to the Piano*, edited by David Rowland (1998); *The Cambridge Companion to the Organ*, edited by Nicholas Thistlethwaite and Geoffrey Webber (1999); *The Cambridge Companion to the Violin* and *The Cambridge Companion to the Cello*, both edited by Robin Stowell (1992; 1999); *The Cambridge Companion to the Clarinet*, edited by Colin Lawson (1995); *The Cambridge Companion to the Saxophone*, edited by Richard Ingham (1999); *The Cambridge Companion to Brass Instruments*, edited by our contributor Trevor Herbert and John Wallace (1997); and *The Cambridge Companion to Singing*, edited by John Potter (2000).

For pianists, a standard work is *The Piano: A History* by Cyril Ehrlich (Oxford: Clarendon Press, 1990); also recommended is *The Book of the Piano*, edited by Dominic Gill (Oxford: Phaidon, 1981). Much detailed evidence about the interpretation of Chopin's piano music is collected in Jean-Jacques Eigeldinger's *Chopin: Pianist and Teacher, as Seen by his Pupils* (Cambridge University Press, 1988). For organists, the standard history, although it is now rather out of date, is William Leslie Sumner's *The Organ: Its Evolution, Principles of Construction and Use*, 4th edn (London: Macdonald and Jane's, 1973).

In addition to his publications listed above, Robin Stowell has written *Violin Technique and Performance Practice in the Late Eighteenth and Early Nineteenth Centuries* (Cambridge University Press, 1990), which has much of interest to players of early Romantic music, and he is the chief contributor to *The Violin Book* (London: Balafon/Outline Press, 1999). Other string instruments are covered in Maurice W. Riley's two-volume *The History of the Viola* (Ann Arbor: Braun-Brumfield, Vol. 1, 2nd edn, 1993; Vol. 2, 1991), *One Hundred Years of Violoncello: A History of Technique and Performance Practice, 1740–1840* by Valerie Walden (Cambridge University Press, 1998), Roslyn Rensch's *The Harp: Its History, Technique and Repertoire* (London: Duckworth, 1969), and Harvey Turnbull's *The Guitar from the Renaissance to the Present Day* (London: Batsford, 1974).

There are two complementary general histories of wind instruments by Anthony Baines: *Woodwind Instruments and their History* (New York: Dover, 1991) and *Brass Instruments: Their History and Development* (New York: Dover, 1993). For players who do not (yet) have their own Cambridge Companions, recommended books are Nancy Toff's *The Flute Book: A Complete Guide for Students and Performers*, 2nd edn (Oxford University Press, 1997), and Günther Joppig's *The Oboe and the Bassoon*, translated by Alfred Clayton (London: Batsford, 1988).

Singers again have a Cambridge Companion, and may also learn a good deal from nineteenth-century treatises. The one by Manuel García has been reprinted in its English translation by Donald V. Paschke as *A Complete Treatise on the Art of Singing* (New York: Da Capo Press, Part I, 1984; Part II, 1975); Nicola Vaccai's *Metodo pratico di canto italiano per camera* is published by Ricordi (Milan: Ricordi, 1990, with English translation).

Yet another useful Cambridge University Press publication is *The Critical Editing of Music: History, Method, and Practice* by James Grier (1996). There is a good selection of facsimiles of composers' manuscripts in *Musical Autographs from Monteverdi to Hindemith*, edited by Emanuel Winternitz (Princeton University Press, 1955; New York: Dover Publications, 1965). Our contributor Robert Pascall has more to say about the processes of editing in his article 'The editor's Brahms', in *The Cambridge Companion to Brahms*, edited by Michael Musgrave (Cambridge University Press, 1999).

Not all the books suggested above are still in print; libraries may have some of them, and may be able to obtain others or suggest alternatives. Don't forget, too, that there is a great deal of information to be obtained from prefaces to editions, notes in CD booklets, magazine articles and Internet websites. But (especially in the case of the Internet) you should always exercise your own judgement about what information is reliable and useful to you – just as you no doubt have done in reading this book.

Notes on the CD

 07.23

Berlioz: *Symphonie fantastique*, fourth movement, *Marche au supplice* (*March to the Scaffold*)

London Classical Players, conductor Sir Roger Norrington

From Virgin Classics VM 5 61379 2, containing Berlioz's complete *Symphonie fantastique* and the overture *Les francs-juges* (licensed courtesy of EMI Marketing)

Berlioz's *Symphonie fantastique*, first performed in Paris in 1830, set the tone for the whole Romantic period, with its graphic storyline, its strong expression of emotion, its freedom from conventions of form and harmony, and its often startling use of a large orchestra. The work describes an artist's obsession with a beautiful girl. In the fourth of the five movements he dreams that he has murdered her, and is being led to the scaffold to be executed for his crime. At the end of the movement the theme which represents the beloved throughout the work (the 'idée fixe') is heard briefly before the guillotine falls. The recording formed part of what Sir Roger Norrington, in his Introduction to this volume, describes as a 'journey' into the nineteenth century with the London Classical Players, using instruments of the period or modern copies. Notice especially the distinctive sonorities of the four bassoons and of the brass section (which includes valved cornets and ophicleides alongside the older instruments), the well-defined pitches of the timpani (played by three drummers), and the clarity of the strings using little or no vibrato.

 03.41

Schumann: Symphony No. 1 in B flat major (Spring), first movement, slow introduction (Andante un poco maestoso) leading to first section of Allegro molto vivace

Orchestre Révolutionnaire et Romantique, conductor Sir John Eliot Gardiner

From Deutsche Grammophon Archiv 457 591-2, a three-disc set including all Schumann's symphonies and some of his other orchestral works

Schumann's First Symphony, which received its premiere in Leipzig in 1841, is a Romantic work in that its symphonic form is combined, though not with a detailed storyline, at least with the poetic idea of spring. This is a recording by another present-day orchestra of period instruments, including natural trumpets and horns; it is notable for its clear colours and general incisiveness of attack. Schumann's score uses many markings of *sf* and > to indicate strong attacks, as well as dynamics of *f* and *ff*: see Clive Brown on pp. 18–19.

 05.13

Brahms: Symphony No. 2 in D major, first movement (Allegro non troppo), first section

Scottish Chamber Orchestra, conductor Sir Charles Mackerras

From Telarc CD-80450, a three-disc set of Brahms's four symphonies and other orchestral works (℗ 1997 Telarc International Corporation)

Brahms's Second Symphony, first performed in Vienna in 1877, is an abstract work in the Classical tradition, but Romantic in its musical language. This recording represents a different approach to stylish performance, using an orchestra of modern instruments, but with the small numbers and layout (first and second violins divided left and right) which Brahms preferred, and conducted with the flexibility of tempo which some musicians claimed he expected – though see Clive Brown on pp. 26–7.

 02.27

Schumann: 'Warum?', No. 3 of *Fantasiestücke* Op. 12

Carl Reinecke (piano roll)

From Archiphon ARC-106, a disc of early piano rolls

Piano rolls, made on special 'reproducing pianos' with extremely sensitive mechanisms, provide valuable evidence of performance traditions before the age of gramophone recording. Carl Reinecke, who knew Mendelssohn and Schumann and was one of the leading conductors and composers in late nineteenth-century Germany, recorded for the Welte-Mignon system late in his long life, in 1905; he is probably the oldest performer of whom we have any kind of recording. Reinecke's performance of Schumann's 'Warum?' ('Why?') shows clearly the rhythmic dislocation between the hands which seems to have typified much Romantic piano playing: see Clive Brown on p. 25.

03.17

Rachmaninoff: Prelude in G flat major, Op. 23 No. 10

Serge Rachmaninoff (piano)

From Philips 456 943-2, a two-disc set in the series Great Pianists of the 20th Century devoted to recordings of Rachmaninoff playing his own and other composers' music

Early 78 rpm gramophone recordings also provide valuable evidence of the Romantic performing style which was still current in the early twentieth century. This recording by the great composer-pianist Rachmaninoff, made in 1940 when he was in his sixties, shows a characteristically Romantic rhythmic freedom, and again a separation of the hands.

 01.43

Mendelssohn: *Songs without Words* Op. 19, No. 2 in A minor

Olga Tverskaya (piano)

From Opus 111 OPS 30-183, a selection of Mendelssohn's *Songs without Words*, played on a copy by David Winston of a fortepiano made by Joseph Brodmann of Vienna in 1823

The original of this instrument is typical of those on which Mendelssohn's *Songs without Words* would have been played as they appeared between 1829 and 1842. The sound may take some getting used to by ears accustomed to the modern piano; but notice the singing tone of the right hand, and the clarity of the left hand even in the deep bass register.

 02.31

Chopin: Mazurka in E minor, Op. 17 No. 2

Janusz Olejniczak (piano)

From Opus 111 OPS 30-286, a Chopin recital played on an original Pleyel piano of 1831

This Chopin mazurka, from a group written in 1832 and '33, is a perfect match for the 1831 Pleyel piano. Notice the delicacy of the upper register, and the clear differentiation between registers. Roy Howat writes about playing Chopin on a Pleyel on p. 36.

 02.57

Debussy: *Préludes* Book 1, *La cathédrale engloutie*, opening

Roy Howat (piano)

From Tall Poppies TP 165, volume 3 of a series of Debussy piano music

Our contributor Roy Howat, a specialist in the music of Debussy, plays the prelude 'The Submerged Cathedral' on a modern piano. See his discussion on p. 38 of the voicing of the opening chords, and of the unmarked tempo variation in bars 7–8, in which he follows the composer's own piano roll.

 03.38

Joachim: Romance in C major

Joseph Joachim (violin), unknown pianist

From Opal CD 9851, containing early recordings of Joachim, Sarasate and Ysaÿe

Joachim, the violinist for whom the Bruch First Concerto, the Dvořák Concerto and the Brahms Concerto were all written, lived long enough to make this recording in 1903, when he was in his seventies. Notice the 'straight', vibratoless tone and the expressive use of portamento, matters discussed by Robin Stowell on pp. 49 and 47–8 respectively. Notice also the flexibility of tempo which Joachim, known as a serious 'classical' player in the tradition of Mendelssohn, considered appropriate for his own salon piece.

 02.51

Brahms (arr. Auer): Hungarian Dance No. 1 in G minor

Leopold Auer (violin), W. Bogutskahein (piano)

From APR CDAPR 7015, a two-disc set which is volume 1 of The Auer Legacy, devoted to recordings by Auer and his pupils

Leopold Auer, the teacher of many of the most celebrated violinists of the twentieth century, including Mischa Elman and Jascha Heifetz, made this private recording in 1920, shortly after giving his seventy-fifth birthday concert. Again, notice the emphasis on portamento as a means of expression, as well as on a great variety of colour. As for vibrato, Auer considered that 'violinists who habitually make use of the device are pitifully misguided' – though, as tastes changed in the first half of the twentieth century, most of his pupils seem to have ignored that advice!

 03.43

Schumann: Romance in A major, Op. 94 No. 2

Fritz Kreisler (violin), Michael Raucheisen (piano)

From Naxos 8.110921 (HNH International Ltd), on which it is a 'filler' for Kreisler's recordings of the Brahms Concerto and Mozart's Fourth Concerto

Fritz Kreisler, one of the leading violinists of the first half of the twentieth century, made this recording of the second of Schumann's Op. 94 Romances (originally designated for oboe) in 1927. Kreisler's playing was of legendary sweetness, the result of his subtle use of portamento and rubato, together with a continuous left-hand vibrato which set the standard for most solo string players of the next generation.

02.45

Saint-Saëns: *The Swan* from *Carnival of the Animals*

Pablo Casals (cello), Nikolai Mednikoff (piano)

From Biddulph LAB 017, containing Casal's recordings for the Victor company in 1927 and '28

Pablo Casals was a role model for twentieth-century cellists, exploring and expanding the repertoire of the instrument and setting new technical standards: his fellow cellist Emanuel Feuermann wrote that he showed 'that the cello can sing without becoming overly sentimental, that phrasing on the cello can be of highest quality'. In this 1928 recording of the famous solo cello movement from Saint-Saëns's 1886 'grand zoological fantasy', notice the use of vibrato, restrained by modern standards and subtly varied, and the expressive use of portamento.

 04.12

Brahms: String Sextet No. 2 in G major, Op. 36, first movement, Allegro non troppo, first section

Hausmusik London

From Signum SIGCD 013, containing the two Brahms sextets (© & ℗ 1999 Signum Records)

The second of Brahms's two sextets for pairs of violins, violas and cellos, written in 1864–5, is played here by a present-day ensemble using instruments and playing techniques appropriate to the period. Notice how the sparing use of vibrato not only clarifies the very full textures but also enhances the expressiveness of Brahms's many semitone clashes.

 03.37

Elgar: 'Enigma' Variations, Theme and Variation I (C.A.E.)

Royal Albert Hall Orchestra, conductor Sir Edward Elgar

From EMI CDM 5 66979 2, a disc in the Great Recordings of the Century series which also includes Elgar's Violin Concerto, played by the young Yehudi Menuhin and again conducted by the composer (licensed courtesy of EMI Marketing)

These are the first two sections of Sir Edward Elgar's 1899 'Enigma' Variations – the theme representing himself and the first variation his wife – from the composer's second recording of the work, made in 1926. This extract shows that even orchestral string players at this time, presumably in a tradition going back well into the nineteenth century, made considerable use of portamento. It also shows Elgar's flexibility of tempo as a conductor: he said that he liked to interpret his music 'elastically and mystically'.

 03.50

Delius: *Brigg Fair*, opening

Symphony orchestra, conductor Sir Thomas Beecham

From BEECHAM 10, a disc in The Beecham Collection devoted to recordings of Delius from the 1920s and '30s

This is the atmospheric opening of Delius's 1907 'English Rhapsody' *Brigg Fair*, based on a Lincolnshire folksong. The recording was conducted by Delius's most trusted interpreter Sir Thomas Beecham at sessions in 1928 and '29. It is included here to show the 'straight' tone adopted by woodwind players of the time, for example the flute in the introduction and the oboe in the first statement of the theme – again presumably in an extension of nineteenth-century tradition. Trevor Herbert discusses wind vibrato on p. 63.

 03.58

Levy: *The Whirlwind Polka*, main section

John Wallace (cornet), The Wallace Collection, conductor Simon Wright

From Nimbus NI 5470 (Nimbus Records), The Origin of the Species, containing music from the repertoire of the mid-nineteenth-century private band at Cyfarthfa Castle in Wales

This is a brilliant display piece for cornet by Jules Levy, who described himself as 'the world's greatest cornet player'. This version is part of the repertoire of the Cyfarthfa Band discovered and edited by Trevor Herbert. The accompanying band plays instruments from the Padbrook Collection of historic brass instruments, including keyed bugles, cornets, saxhorns and ophicleides. See pp. 61–2 for Trevor Herbert's discussion of nineteenth-century brass band music and the appropriate playing style for it.

 03.17

Bellini: *La sonnambula*, aria 'Ah! non credea'

Adelina Patti (soprano), Alfredo Barili (piano), recorded 1906

From Nimbus NI 7840/1 (Nimbus Records), a two-disc set of early recordings of many singers, called The Era of Adelina Patti

The celebrated soprano Adelina Patti was sixty-three when she recorded this aria of the sleep-walking Amina in Bellini's 1831 opera *La sonnambula* – the role in which she had made her European operatic début forty-five years earlier. See David Mason's discussion of Patti's use of decoration on p. 77.

03.20

Brahms: *Feldeinsamkeit*, Op. 86 No. 2

Gustav Walter (tenor), unknown pianist

From an HMV transfer of a recording made in 1904, not currently available (licensed courtesy of EMI Marketing)

This recording, by a singer whom Brahms knew and apparently approved of, is transcribed as Ex. 6.14 and discussed by David Mason on p. 86. The song, published in 1882, describes the poet's feelings as he lies alone in the fields, looking up at the sky; he imagines himself long dead, and drifting like the clouds through the heavens. (This recording is in the key of A major; the song was originally published for low voice in F major, as shown in Ex. 6.14.)

 02.56

Smetana: *Dalibor*, aria 'Blickst du mein Freund'

Hermann Winkelmann (tenor), unknown pianist

From an HMV transfer of a recording made in 1905, not currently available (licensed courtesy of EMI Marketing)

As David Mason says on p. 86, Hermann Winkelmann was the oldest Wagnerian tenor to make recordings – though unfortunately they did not include any Wagner. His heroic but also soulful style (and his very clear diction) can be heard in this aria from Smetana's 1868 opera *Dalibor*, originally in Czech but sung here in German (with piano accompaniment). In fifteenth-century Prague, the hero Dalibor is on trial for killing an aristocrat in revenge for the execution of his friend Zdeněk; condemned to life imprisonment, he has a vision of his friend waiting for him in heaven.

 02.25

Bellini: *I puritani*, 'Qui la voce'

Maria Callas (soprano), unidentified orchestra and conductor

From Nimbus NI 7864 (Nimbus Records), More Legendary Voices, an anthology of great singers of the past

Maria Callas is generally considered the twentieth-century singer who most completely exemplifies the bel canto tradition. This recording from early in her career shows her control of legato and portamento, and her precision in even the most exacting coloratura passages. The aria 'O rendetemi', from Bellini's *I puritani* of 1835, is sung by Elvira when, thinking she has been abandoned by her betrothed, she goes mad; in this final section, she imagines herself at their wedding feast.